SIERRA LEONE
Healthcare Workers' Perspectives
on their
MENTAL HEALTH
during the
EBOLA
OUTBREAK

HOW IT CAN BE STOPPED

GUY TAYLOR, PhD.

Order this book online at www.trafford.com
or email orders@trafford.com

Most Trafford titles are also available at major online book retailers.

© Copyright 2019 Guy Taylor, PhD.

All rights reserved. No part of this publication may be reproduced, stored in a retrieval system, or transmitted, in any form or by any means, electronic, mechanical, photocopying, recording, or otherwise, without the written prior permission of the author.

Print information available on the last page.

ISBN: 978-1-4907-9633-8 (sc)
ISBN: 978-1-4907-9634-5 (hc)
ISBN: 978-1-4907-9637-6 (e)

Library of Congress Control Number: 2019910082

Because of the dynamic nature of the Internet, any web addresses or links contained in this book may have changed since publication and may no longer be valid. The views expressed in this work are solely those of the author and do not necessarily reflect the views of the publisher, and the publisher hereby disclaims any responsibility for them.

Any people depicted in stock imagery provided by Getty Images are models, and such images are being used for illustrative purposes only.
Certain stock imagery © Getty Images.

Trafford rev. 07/24/2019

 www.trafford.com

North America & international
toll-free: 1 888 232 4444 (USA & Canada)
fax: 812 355 4082

Walden University

College of Social and Behavioral Sciences

This is to certify that the doctoral dissertation by
Guy Taylor

has been found to be complete and satisfactory in all
respects, and that any and all revisions required by
the review committee have been made.

Review Committee
Dr. Patricia Loun, Committee Chairperson, Psychology Faculty
Dr. Jay Greiner, Committee Member, Psychology Faculty
Dr. Yoly Zentella, University Reviewer, Psychology Faculty

Chief Academic Officer
Eric Riedel, Ph.D.

Walden University
2019

Perspectives of Sierra Leoneans Healthcare Workers'
Mental Health During the Ebola Outbreak

by
Guy Taylor

Dissertation Submitted in Partial Fulfillment of the
Requirements for the Degree of Doctor of Philosophy
Clinical Psychology

Walden University
May 2019

The mental health of healthcare workers during the Ebola outbreak in West Africa was a serious concern for healthcare professionals and the mental health field. One area in West Africa where healthcare workers played a significant role during the Ebola outbreak of 2014 and 2015 was Sierra Leone. This qualitative research study was designed to explore the perceptions of Sierra Leoneans healthcare workers' mental health, how they coped, and treatment they received while providing care for Ebola virus patients. This study, with a phenomenological research approach, used purposeful sampling to recruit 10 healthcare workers to participate in semi structured, open-ended interviews. The stress theory model and a hermeneutic phenomenology conceptual framework were used as a lens of analysis to understand the views of healthcare workers who worked directly with Ebola virus patients in Freetown, Sierra Leone. The results of the analysis of the collected data produced 9 major themes. The major themes suggest that healthcare workers experienced mental health symptoms such as depression and anxiety, personal thoughts and feelings such as insomnia, and suicidal ideation. Strategies for coping included using the Bible; and the detrimental impact included facing discrimination after the Ebola outbreak. Most of the healthcare workers blame the government for not providing adequate coping resources, which led to the personal consequence of hopelessness. This study may benefit mental health professionals working in an epidemic. Additionally, this study may contribute to social change by providing a deeper understanding of the mental health system and healthcare workers in Freetown, Sierra Leone.

Perspectives of Sierra Leoneans Healthcare Workers'
Mental Health During the Ebola Outbreak

by
Guy Taylor

Dissertation Submitted in Partial Fulfillment of the
Requirements for the Degree of Doctor of Philosophy
Clinical Psychology

Walden University
August 2019

INFORMATION TO ALL USERS

The quality of this reproduction is dependent
upon the quality of the copy submitted.

Contents

Dedication xxi
Acknowledgments xxiii

Chapter 1   Introduction to the Study 1
Chapter 2   Literature Review 17
Chapter 3   Research Method 54
Chapter 4   Result 69
Chapter 5   Discussion, Recommendations, and Conclusions 85

References 101
Appendix A Invitation Letter 119
Appendix B Interview Questions 123
Appendix C Human Subject Training Certificate 125

List of Tables

Table 1	Demographics of the Participants	70
Table 2	Themes and Codes Related to HCWs' Mental Health	79
Table 3	Themes and Codes Related to HCWs' Coping	81
Table 4	Themes and Codes Related to HCWs' Treatment	82

List of Figures

Figure 1 Health care workers' occupations—Cases by attribute value. 71

Figure 2 Health care workers' tribes—Cases by attribute value. 71

Dedication

This dissertation is dedicated to my late mother, Minnie Oyedele Macauley, who taught me that fame is the food that the dead eat. She also taught me that honesty is the best policy in the world. This dissertation is also dedicated to all the Ebola victims and the HCWs who put their lives on the line to help ordinary people who were infected with the Ebola virus. Also, this dissertation is dedicated to my children, Guy JR and Jermel, who did not understand what I was doing during the time I was studying and researching in my quiet corner at my home. I also dedicate this book to all of my family members, including my brother Leslie Taylor and my late brother Oliver May-Cole, who gave me an opportunity to come to the United States to pursue my studies. Also, to all the people who showed me empathy during my struggle to attain this goal. Once again, to my late mother, who reminded me when I was a young boy that the height of success was never attained by sudden flight but by perseverance and hard work.

Acknowledgments

I will always acknowledge the presence of God, who gave me the strength and wisdom to continue this journey. Dr. Loun, who challenged me on areas in which I was struggling; through her guidance and dedication, I was able to attain my goal. I also want to thank Dr. Greiner as my committee member who agreed to be part of my study and guide me through the process. Dr. Zentella, my URR, who showed interest in my work and provided me with effective feedback in a timely manner. I also want to personally thank Walden University for giving me an opportunity to effect positive social change not only in the United States, but also in West Africa. As I continue this journey, I am committed to making a difference in the world. As one of my professors from Walden University told me, "Complete your degree, get your license, and change the world."

CHAPTER 1

Introduction to the Study

Introduction

Healthcare workers (HCWs) in an epidemic experience mental health problems. HCWs with inadequate mental health care experienced mental health difficulties during the 2014 and 2015 Ebola virus disease (EVD) outbreak (Bell, 2016; World Health Organization [WHO], 2016). The mental health delivery system in Westernized countries provides effective mental health services to HCWs during an epidemic; however, this is not the case in West African nations (Coltart, Johnson, &Whitty, 2015). West African nations such as Sierra Leone continue to provide an inadequate mental health delivery system for HCWs (Delamou, Beavogui, Konde, van Griensven, & De Brouwere, 2015; Eckes, 2016). Cheung (2015) indicated that HCWs during the EVD outbreak in West Africa experienced unexplained psychological symptoms. Cheung called for effective mental health care in West Africa. Qualitative studies have indicated that first responders such as HCWs are prone to suffer posttraumatic stress disorder (PTSD) and significant psychological trauma during an epidemic (Paladino et al., 2017). While studies have assessed mental health symptoms via quantitative instruments (Betancourt et al., 2016; Khalid, Khalid, &Qabajah, 2016; Li et al., 2015), they have not been able to address the subjective experience of mental health care or symptoms that HCWs experienced during the Ebola virus outbreak, which would provide more meaningful, in-depth, and helpful information on their mental health symptoms during the EVD epidemic.

Objective assessments have indicated that HCWs during the EVD outbreak experienced mental health symptoms and stress. However, objective assessments do not know what kind of symptoms they experienced or if they personally felt that they were suffering because all of the quantitative studies used objective assessments and not subjective ones. Further, researchers know that the mental health care system in West Africa was inadequate. Researchers do not know if HCWs sought help, or if that help was available and effective.

This qualitative research study was conducted to explore HCWs' perspectives on their mental health symptoms and lived experiences during the Ebola outbreak and to help address problems of the current mental health system in Sierra Leone. This study would also help to address public policies related to HCWs' perspectives on their mental health during an epidemic.

The rest of this chapter includes background information on HCWs' mental health and the mental health care system in Freetown, Sierra Leone; the statement of the problem; the nature of the study; the purpose of the study; and the research question for this study. I also discuss the theoretical framework and conceptual framework that were used in this study. Furthermore, I explain the assumptions, scope of delimitations, and limitations of the study. Finally, I conclude with the significance of the study and a summary of this chapter.

Background

HCWs with inadequate mental health care are unable to cope with stress that leads to mental health difficulties when working with highly infectious patients. Although most of the literature in Chapter 2 addressed the need for effective mental health treatment for HCWs, mental health specialists in West Africa have been unsuccessful in their efforts to provide quality mental healthcare for HCWs. In fact, Bell (2016), WHO (2016), and Mugisha, De Hert, Stubbs, Basangwa, and Vancampfort (2017) stressed the importance of quality mental healthcare for HCWs in West Africa during an epidemic. It happens that the advocacy for effective mental health treatment for HCWs in West Africa has not been effective. Betancourt et al. (2016), Hughes

(2015), and Li et al. (2015) postulated that the mental health system in West Africa is either nonexistent or inadequate.

Several studies have called for effective mental health treatment for HCWs in Africa (Centers for Disease Control and Prevention [CDC], 2014; WHO, 2016); other studies have also noted that the lack of effective mental health treatment in Africa for HCWs may affect the mental health of HCWs (Gwaikolo, Kohrt, & Cooper, 2017; Mugisha et al., 2017). According to Li et al. (2015), Scott et al. (2009), and Ansumana et al. (2017), HCWs in Africa experience mixed mental health symptoms that need to be studied. Mental health is still a serious problem in Africa that should be addressed by qualified healthcare professionals (Hughes, 2015). It is made clear in the literature review that there are limited intervention measures for mental health in Africa. However, the limited intervention techniques used in Africa appeared to be ineffective to address HCWs' mental health symptoms during the 2014 and 2015 EVD outbreak. Lund, Myer, Stein, Williams, and Flisher (2013); Greenberg, Wessely, and Wykes (2015);and Brolin Ribacke et al. (2016) postulated that one of the major reasons that mental health care is inaccessible to HCWs is lack of government assistance.

Jalloh et al. (2018) and WHO (2015) postulated that HCWs exhibited psychological symptoms after they experienced the death of 26,277 HCWs during the Ebola outbreak. Additional studies have indicated that lack of adequate resources induces stress among HCWs during an epidemic (Moll, 2014; Selamu, Thornicroft, Fekadu, &Hanlon, 2017). HCWs who did not have effective coping skills during the epidemic experienced tremendous stress (Khalid et al., 2016).

While the poor mental health of HCWs may affect their occupational abilities, the long-term impact of mental health difficulties may lead them to substance abuse problems (Mokaya et al., 2016). HCWs may experience occupational stress and burnout due to lack of social support, which may lead to mental illness (Glasberg, Eriksson, &Norberg, 2007). Musa, John, Habib, and Kuznik (2016) and deMenil, Knapp, McDaid, and Njenga (2014) argued that high economic cost and high unemployment are among the reasons why mental health treatment in Africa is ineffective. There could be a serious mental health crisis among HCWs if their mental health is not addressed (CDC, 2014; Konis et al., 2015; WHO, 2016). These studies together confirmed that HCWs with mental illness might have difficulties in living a normal life. Currently, the body of literature addressing this problem in West Africa is limited (Hughes, 2015; WHO, 2016).

Problem Statement

The mental health of HCWs who cared for patients with the Ebola virus in 2014 in West Africa has received little or no attention from healthcare professionals. Much of the scholarly research on HCWs during the EVD outbreak has focused on the physiological health of HCWs (WHO, 2016) and not on their mental health (Greenberg et al., 2015). The WHO (2016) continues to educate people about the need for mental healthcare for HCWs in the West African region after the Ebola virus epidemic. HCWs make good decisions and provide quality care for their patients when they have good mental health (Rugema et al., 2015). HCWs have experienced the death of over 26,277 confirmed cases of Ebola victims in Sierra Leone, Guinea, and Liberia (WHO, 2016).

According to WHO (2016), some of these Ebola victims were related to the HCWs. Different stressors can affect HCWs' mental health and their work performance (WHO, 2016). HCWs in West Africa have a 5% higher chance than others of becoming infected with EVD (Petti, Protano, Messano, & Scully, 2016).

In a qualitative study not related to the EVD outbreak, Scott et al. (2009) indicated that HCWs are second victims, especially when they watch their clients die. Engel et al. (2017) conducted a qualitative study on a diagnostic practice for HIV patients in South Africa. They found that information provided by HCWs was relevant to implementing better strategies to help HCWs and the general population.

In a qualitative study, Hughes (2015) indicated that there would be an increase in psychiatric morbidity among HCWs treating EVD patients in West Africa because of the lack of proper mental health care for them. The WHO (2014) noted that the lack of qualified mental health professionals in Sierra Leone had increased psychological distress among HCWs who treated EVD patients. Greenberg et al. (2015) indicated that it is imperative that scientists find an effective treatment for EVD and stressed that the psychological needs of HCWs and patients should not be ignored.

Based on the existing data, quantitative studies conducted by researchers have indicated that HCWs experience anxiety, depression, and PTSD (Li et al., 2015; Scott et al., 2009). Some of the research has indicated that HCWs suffer specific symptoms while some studies have not found that HCWs are distressed (Khalid et al., 2016; Koh et al., 2015). Therefore, the extent of mental health issues among HCWs treating patients with EVD is unknown. To better understand HCWs' lived experiences in relation to their mental health while providing treatment to patients with the Ebola virus in Sierra Leone, I conducted a qualitative study. While numerous studies have examined the medical aspects of the Ebola virus, no qualitative study has been done to examine the perspectives of HCWs in Sierra Leone on experiencing mental health symptoms while providing treatment to patients with EVD. While researchers know from a quantitative study (Cheung, 2015; Scott et al., 2009) that HCWs experienced anxiety, depression, and PTSD, the qualitative perspective in the current study adds to knowledge about mental health issues of HCWs who treat patients with the Ebola virus. A qualitative inquiry into HCWs' mental status and perceived stressors while providing treatment to patients with the Ebola virus provided relevant information that may lead to quality mental health care interventions for the next EVD outbreak. This study addressed gaps in the literature about how HCWs related to their mental health status while providing treatment to patients with EVD during the EVD outbreak in Freetown, Sierra Leone.

Purpose of the Study

The purpose of this study was to use a qualitative approach to explore the lived experiences of HCWs in Freetown, Sierra Leone involving mental health symptoms while providing treatment to patients with EVD. The rationale for conducting this study was to provide more meaningful, in-depth, and helpful information on mental health symptoms experienced by HCWs during the EVD outbreak. This study may also foster positive social change that enables HCWs and mental health professionals to work together to address the mental health crisis in Freetown, Sierra Leone.

The interpretivist paradigm is often used in qualitative studies. According to Cohen and Manion (1994), interpretive researchers seek to understand the world of human experience. This finding gives credence to Creswell's (2009) contention that interpretivist researchers understand the world through participants' points of view, backgrounds, and experiences. The interpretivist paradigm was used in this study because it enabled HCWs in Freetown, Sierra Leone to describe their mental illness symptoms when working with highly infectious patients.

Research Questions

This study was conducted to understand and explore the lived experiences of HCWs in Freetown, Sierra Leone. This inquiry facilitated a greater understanding of HCWs' mental health during the EVD outbreak. I employed thoughtful consideration of the topic and a thorough review of pieces of literature related to the topic, which enabled me to formulate the following research questions:

> RQ1. How do HCWs in Sierra Leone describe their lived experiences regarding their own mental health when treating patients with Ebola virus disease?
>
> RQ2. How do HCWs feel about their abilities to cope with stress while treating patients with the Ebola virus disease?
>
> RQ3. How do HCWs describe their lived experiences of the mental health care treatment they received while treating patients with the Ebola virus disease?

Theoretical Framework

The stress process model was most appropriate for this study because it is useful in explaining and identifying the stress factors that contribute to mental health illness. The stress process model is used to understand stress factors contributing to well-being.

Pearlin, Morton, Lieberman, Menaghan, and Mullan (1981) were the first to use the stress process model to give some conceptual organization to a diverse line of research. There are several factors intertwined with the idea of well-being: "the social status of the individual," "the context that envelopes daily lives," and individuals' "exposures to stressors, and resources that they can use to respond to the stressors, and the way stress is manifested in their psychological and bodily functioning" (Pearlin, 1989, p.396). Pearlin (1989) indicated that these stress factors are interconnected, in that what affects one stress factor can affect the other stress factors. According to Pearlin, social stress is found among ordinary people who are involved in everyday activities.

Aneshensel (1992) postulated that mental disorders could be caused by different stressors. According to Pearlin (1989), psychologists and psychiatrists are concerned with mental health outcomes when people are under stress. I used the stress process model to explore the stressors of HCWs while treating patients with EVD. According to Pearlin et al. (1981), three factors contribute to the stress process model: stressors, moderation and mediation, and stress outcomes. Pearlin argued that stressors coming from external environmental factors can force a person to be exposed to unwanted events. Moderation and mediation are social and personal factors that modulate the effect of certain stressors. Stress outcomes include the following: emotional distress, psychological distress, anxiety, and other psychosocial distress (Pearlin, 1999).

The use of the stress process model was appropriate for this study because it brought forth the views of HCWs in Freetown, Sierra Leone on how they perceived the stress factors involved when taking care of patients with EVD. Phenomenology was appropriate because this method enabled participants to share their lived experiences of their own mental health when treating patients with EVD. Further explanation regarding the stress process model and phenomenology is shared in Chapter 2. This theory related to the study approach and research questions because it helped to explain the behavior and attitudes of HCWs during the EVD outbreak. This theory also helped to explain how stress affects HCWs treating patients with the EVD.

Conceptual Framework

HCWs' perceptions of their mental health constituted the phenomenon that grounded this study. I used Heidegger's (1889) conceptual framework of hermeneutic phenomenology to understand the mental illness that HCWs experienced while providing treatment to highly infectious patients. Phenomenology methodology was originated by Husserl (1982). However, Heidegger (1992) was a student of Husserl, and he formulated the concept of a hermeneutic or interpretive approach to phenomenology (Converse, 2012; Peredaryenko& Krauss, 2013). In this naturalistic qualitative phenomenological study, I explored the lived experiences of HCWs involving their mental health during the Ebola outbreak in Freetown, Sierra Leone. The conceptual framework of hermeneutic phenomenology has been used to understand the lived experiences of various phenomena (Tuohy, Cooney, Dowling, Murphy, & Sixsmith, 2013; Valandra, 2012). Further explanation regarding hermeneutic phenomenological studies of HCWs is presented in Chapter 2.

Mental illness is a serious concern among HCWs working with highly infectious patients (Li et al., 2015; Scott et al., 2009). Pescosolido(2013) postulated that individuals with mental illness are labeled based on their appearance and their socioeconomic status. Pescosolido recognized that a mental illness diagnosis creates discrimination and prejudice. Researchers have indicated that phenomenology involves how individuals experience various phenomena, including ways of seeing, knowing about, and having skills related to such phenomena (Patton, 2002). Heidegger (1992) indicated that the aim of phenomenology is to qualitatively discover different ways that individuals experience, conceptualize, realize, and understand aspects of phenomena in an environment. Patton (2002) also stated that a researcher can make a meaningful theoretical contribution by observing a phenomenon that does not have a name and then giving it a name. Thus, I found that the perspectives of HCWs in Freetown, Sierra Leone could help in formulating a hypothesis regarding better mental health interventions for HCWs. Other researchers such as Shane (2007) have described hermeneutic phenomenology as studying the awareness and reflections of participants.

The conceptual framework of hermeneutic phenomenology related to this study approach because it enabled me to employ an inductive approach (Patton, 2002) and answer the key research question—How do HCWs in Sierra Leone describe their lived experiences regarding their own mental health? In addition, the conceptual framework of hermeneutic phenomenology enabled me to start with the data to make sense of the lived experiences of HCWs and their perspectives on their own mental health. Hermeneutic phenomenology was used as a conceptual framework to explore HCWs' mental health while providing treatment to patients with the EVD in Freetown, Sierra Leone. Because stress and mental health were used interchangeably, Pearlin's stress process model theory and hermeneutic phenomenology provided the framework for this study.

Nature of the Study

I used a qualitative phenomenological approach to explore the phenomenon of interest. I explored the lived experiences of HCWs from Sierra Leone about their mental health as it related to stress during the EVD outbreak, including their perceptions, beliefs, and attitudes while treating patients with EVD. Qualitative interviewing enabled me to begin with the assumption that HCWs' experiences were meaningful and could be made explicit (Patton, 2002). Creswell (2009) indicated that the phenomenological design focuses on the essence of a lived experience. Morse (2006) noted that individuals may have different opinions on similar experiences.

Husserl (1982) indicated that a sample size of 10 could be assessed in a qualitative research. This sample size was estimated based on the approach of the study, which was phenomenology. Morse (1994) postulated that qualitative sample sizes should be large enough to obtain feedback for most or all perceptions. In phenomenological studies, Creswell (2009) indicated that five to 25 participants are enough, whereas Morse suggested at least six participants.

The HCWs who participated in this study were registered nurses and a psychiatrist between the ages of 36 and 60 years who were currently working at Connaught Hospital in Freetown, Sierra Leone. The target population in this study consisted of two women and eight men who were originally from Sierra Leone and were working as

HCWs. According to estimate, all 150 of the HCWs (nurses and a psychiatrist) were employed during the EVD outbreak (Hughes, 2015). I recruited 10 participants from within this population.

I used purposeful sampling for this study. Purposeful sampling is used in qualitative research to obtain information from a population (Patton, 2002). Purposeful sampling enabled me to select members of a group who had knowledge of the phenomenon of interest. The participants' ethnicities were Creole, Mende, Temne, and Limba. All of the participants spoke English, which is the official language in Sierra Leone, as well as a common language called Krio.

I conducted a recorded interview of approximately 45 minutes with each participant. I developed a set of open-ended questions related to the research questions. The data were analyzed by using the analysis of statements gathered during the interview. Moustakas (1994) indicated that the gathering of information in phenomenology is called an *essence description*. I used NVivo10 to analyze the data. NVivo 10 software enables researchers to sort and arrange their files. Coding was used as a method of developing themes that emerged from the interview/transcript. Most of my data were managed using software, index cards, and sticky notes. The data were collected in Freetown, Sierra Leone.

Definition of Terms

Epidemic: The spread of a disease in different areas or among a specific group of people (WHO, 2013).

Healthcare worker (HCW): A person whose job description is to help and protect the well-being of people and communities (WHO, 2015).

Anxiety disorders: A group of mental disorders that produce a feeling of restlessness and fear (American Psychiatric Association [APA], 2013).

Mental health: A condition that describes a person's psychological and emotional well-being (APA, 2013).

Depression: A persistent feeling of sadness and worthlessness that results in a lack of desire to engage in activities that were once pleasurable (APA, 2013).

Middle East respiratory syndrome (MERS): A respiratory illness that is recognized in a person (WHO, 2015).

Phobic anxiety: Fear of an object or a situation (APA, 2013).

Paranoid ideation: A grandiose belief that one is being persecuted, harassed, or treated unfairly (APA, 2013).

Interpersonal sensitivity: The ability to judge someone correctly (Brew& Kottler, 2008).

Posttraumatic stress disorder (PTSD): May affect anyone who has been exposed to a traumatic or a stressful event (APA, 2013).

Paradigm: A set of beliefs or assumptions (Patton, 2002).

Assumptions

Creswell (2009) and Frankfort-Nachmias and Nachmias (2008) stated that researchers must be aware of assumptions when conducting a study. Creswell (2009) indicated that researchers bring their beliefs and their philosophical assumptions to a study. In a quantitative study, there is a hypothesis. However, in a qualitative study, there is no hypothesis. For this qualitative study, I had five assumptions in my mind. These assumptions were as follows:

- I assumed that all of the participants in the study would remain truthful.
- I assumed that HCWs understood the need for an effective mental health care system in Freetown, Sierra Leone.
- I assumed that HCWs in Freetown, Sierra Leone wanted to know if they had any mental illness.
- I assumed that the interview questions would enable me to collect the correct information for the study.
- I assumed that the result of the study would effect positive social change.

Scope and Delimitations

The mental health of HCWs in Freetown, Sierra Leone during the EVD epidemic has been a serious concern for mental health care professionals. The literature review indicated that mental healthcare intervention for HCWs is inadequate (Betancourt et al., 2016; Greenberg et al., 2015; Hughes, 2015). There has been a need to explore HCWs' perspectives on their mental health during the Ebola virus outbreak in order to provide effective measures for mental health treatment in Freetown, Sierra Leone. The scope of the study was limited to HCWs and did not encompass other individuals who might have been involved in caretaking. Enabling HCWs in the West African region to voice their opinions empowered them as they shared insights on the mental health symptoms they experienced.

During an epidemic, HCWs may experience the loss of patients, friends, and family members. It was important to select HCWs as participants in this study because they could provide vital information on the topic of interest. They were able to relay information related to the direct and indirect mental health symptoms they had experienced while providing care for highly infectious patients. Further, in reviewing additional literature, it became obvious that how HCWs coped with stress during the Ebola virus epidemic had not been fully studied.

I selected Pearlin et al.'s (1981) stress process model as the best theory for the study and Heidegger's (1889) hermeneutic phenomenology as a conceptual model. The stress process model was chosen over its counterpart, the ecological model, because it explains and identifies the stress factors that contribute to mental health issues. The stress process model was able to bring forth the views of HCWs on how they perceived intervention measures for stress and mental health intervention that were used during the Ebola virus outbreak. As such, the stress process model was optimal for the study.

Though ecological theory is highly related to this area of study, its main focus is on various systems of human development (Bronfenbrenner, 1994). Barrera (2011) conducted a study on how individuals view various mental health systems in their environments (Barrera, 2011). Barrera used the ecological system to understand why Latinos were not accessing the mental health system available to them. Barrera found that microsystems played a significant role in how individuals viewed the mental health system. In another study, the ecological system was used by McCall (2009) for the examination of school human development. McCall concluded that learning and health are determined by the interaction of individuals in various systems of the environment. I did not select this theory because this study was built on HCWs' perspectives on their mental health and how they coped with stress. Ecological theory would have been optimal if this study had been focused on the efforts of public health (as a macrosystem) to eliminate EVD.

Pearlin (1999) asserted that there are several factors associated with well-being. Applying Pearlin's theory, I sought to guide HCWs to describe their experiences with mental health professionals with an aim toward developing adequate mental health care for HCWs in Freetown, Sierra Leone. Furthermore, using an approach informed by Husserl's phenomenology, I prompted HCWs to elaborate on the mental illness they had experienced during the EVD outbreak.

Because the study was qualitative, I considered boundaries when interviewing participants. In a qualitative study, the physical proximity between the interviewer and the participants must be taken seriously. The scope and delimitations enabled me to reach authentic findings through the study. This study was delimited to (a) HCWs in Freetown, Sierra Leone;(b) HCWs who had worked directly or indirectly with EVD patients; and(c) participants who understood and spoke fluent English.

Limitations

Qualitative methodology has its limitations, which should be considered when conducting a study. Creswell (2009) asserted that quantitative and qualitative research have different methodological approaches. Creswell pointed out that qualitative research involves both credibility and trustworthiness. According to Cope (2014), credibility in qualitative research can be supported by researchers' ability to engage in the right methods when conducting the study. Polit and Beck (2006) emphasized that credibility includes the truth of the data being studied and the researchers' truthfulness in the interpretation of the data. Sandelowski (1986) pointed out that the credibility of a study is based on the recognition of the phenomenon by other people who share the same experience being studied. Polit and Beck (2006) asserted for a study to remain reliable, it must have credibility and trustworthiness. Guba and Lincoln (1994) indicated that reliability and validity are intertwined with trustworthiness in a qualitative study. In addition, trustworthiness and quality can only be maintained when a study is reliable, transferable, dependable, and credible (Cope, 2014). Therefore, credibility and reliability are imperative in a qualitative study.

Creswell (2009) indicated that researchers are responsible for taking the right steps to maintain accuracy and credibility in their findings. To provide credibility and trustworthiness to this study. I employed the strategies of both qualitative validity and reliability. These strategies were as follows:

- As a single researcher, I employed an intercoder. According to Creswell (2009), intercoder agreement occurs when two or more coders agree on the codes used for a study.
- I carefully examined evidence from the sources gathered to justify the themes.
- I conducted a follow-up interview with participants to get feedback on the findings.
- I used peer debriefing to foster accuracy of the study.

As an active participant in the study, my participation could have led to bias. Therefore, I anticipated the following limitations:

- I was born in Freetown, Sierra Leone, which might have fostered bias and prejudice due to my knowledge of the environment and the participants.
- I only targeted a sample population of HCWs in Freetown, which could be considered a limited sample.
- The result or outcomes of the study may be called into question because all participants were HCWs in the Western area of Freetown, Sierra Leone.
- The sample population might not generalize to other populations in Freetown, Sierra Leone.

Significance

This study was significant because HCWs in Freetown, Sierra Leone may have experienced mental health problems during the 2014 and 2015 Ebola outbreak (Li et al., 2015; WHO, 2016). EVD continues to be a healthcare concern in West Africa. Western countries have found an effective strategy to provide mental health care during epidemics like the EVD outbreak; this has not been the case for mental health care in West African nations. The latest incident of the EVD happened in Sierra Leone in 2016, after Sierra Leone was discovered an Ebola-free country (WHO, 2016). Additional studies have indicated that health care workers and family members of HCWs who had contact with infected people were at higher risk for EVD than individuals who had no contact with infected patients (WHO, 2016). Further, pregnant women with EVD were at risk of passing EVD to their unborn children. These factors may have increased stress for HCWs (WHO, 2014). Aneshensel (1992) argued that mental disorders can be caused by stress. Intervention methods to combat the Ebola virus involve education, handwashing, avoiding patients infected with the virus, and avoiding dead bodies with the virus (Eckes, 2016). Despite these interventions, EVD continues to be a threat to HCWs, and HCWs continue to experience mental health difficulties related to EVD.

This study provided opportunities for HCWs to understand their mental health symptoms. It also provided opportunities for mental healthcare professionals and the general Sierra Leone population to understand the signs and symptoms of mental illness. Additionally, this study was significant because Sierra Leoneans think that the EVD epidemic might reoccur in West Africa. This study examined the beliefs of HCWs in Sierra Leone to gain a more in-depth understanding of their mental health during the EVD outbreak.

It is important that HCWs tell their stories to inform policymakers and practitioners, especially those in the mental healthcare delivery system, so that they can implement better interventions in case there is another outbreak of EVD. The views of HCWs may contribute to social change, which may lead to the implementation of better mental health treatment interventions, mental health clinics, and improved mental health education related to EVD or any epidemic. Knowing the views of HCWs may encourage Sierra Leoneans to become advocates for a high-quality psychological health care system for workers dealing with EVD and other infectious diseases. The information provided in this study may promote positive social change and awareness of the mental health crisis, and it may help mental health care workers to feel empowered.

Summary

The WHO (2016) and various researchers (Coltart et al., 2015; Jalloh et al., 2018) have recognized that the mental health of HCWs in West Africa during an epidemic should not be ignored. The 2014 and 2015 Ebola outbreak in West Africa affected the mental health of HCWs. The WHO (2016) indicated that early diagnosis of mental health issues in HCWs would enable them to receive effective mental healthcare. HCWs mostly suffer from mental health problems during an epidemic because of the enormous stress of their roles as first responders (Gustafsson, Norberg, & Stranberg, 2008; Li et al., 2015). Mental health care professionals and researchers have advocated tirelessly for an adequate mental health system in Africa (CDC, 2014; WHO, 2016).

The efforts of researchers and healthcare professionals to establish an adequate mental health system in Africa have failed. Understanding the views of HCWs in Freetown, Sierra Leone on the mental health symptoms that they experienced could enable mental health officials to start a dialogue that might promote an efficient mental health system in Freetown, Sierra Leone.

This study is important because it provides relevant information on the mental health symptoms of HCWs during the EVD epidemic. It may also enable HCWs to voice their opinions on how increased stress during an epidemic could cause mental illness and how it could also affect their work performance.

CHAPTER 2

Literature Review

Introduction

After the Ebola virus outbreak in West Africa in 2014, the mental health of HCWs was the focus of increased interest in the healthcare field. Within the last couple of years of the EVD epidemic, the HCWs of Sierra Leone received humanitarian help from the CDC (Johnson, 2014). The CDC (2014) and Li et al. (2015) found that HCWs in Sierra Leone were unable to cope with stress while treating patients with EVD, resulting in anxiety, depression, and PTSD. Ansumana et al. (2017) indicated that HCWs in Sierra Leone experienced a feeling of loneliness and isolation during the EVD outbreak. There has been a need to study HCWs' mental health symptoms in Freetown, Sierra Leone because of the evidence that they were affected mentally during the EVD outbreak of 2014 to 2015.

The WHO (2016) postulated that little is known about the severity of mental health issues in impoverished nations such as Sierra Leone. The CDC (2014) has indicated that numerous attempts to provide adequate mental health treatments in the African nation have effectively failed. To date, numerous studies have investigated whether HCWs have received adequate mental health treatment, especially during an outbreak of a disease such as EVD (CDC, 2014; Hughes, 2015; WHO, 2016). Studies have found that mental health treatment in this context has been nonexistent or ineffective (Betancourt et al., 2016; WHO, 2015). Raab, Sogge, Parker, and Flament (2015) and

WHO (2016) addressed the need for good mental health among HCWs while providing care for their clients to help address any mental health difficulties they might be experiencing. The lack of adequate mental health treatment for HCWs may result from the poor availability of mental health care in Sierra Leone more generally. HCWs are not the only ones affected by inadequate mental health treatment in West Africa; their families, friends, and clients can also be affected by inadequate mental health care (CDC, 2014; WHO, 2014). Research has also postulated that limited psychotropic medications, lack of well-trained clinicians, and high turnover contribute to inadequate mental health treatment in Sierra Leone (Gwaikolo et al., 2017; WHO, 2016). The WHO (2016) has called for more attention to be paid to the mental health system in West Africa. The WHO (2016) indicated that mental illness is a serious problem among the general population in West Africa.

Additional qualitative studies are needed to find effective mental health care for HCWs. Numerous studies have provided information on the medical aspect of the Ebola virus among HCWs. Based on existing data, quantitative studies conducted by researchers have indicated that HCWs have experienced anxiety, depression, and PTSD (Ansumana et al., 2017; Cheung, 2015; Li et al., 2015; Scott et al., 2009). However, no qualitative study has been conducted related to the mental health aspect of HCWs' experiences in Sierra Leone while providing care for patients with EVD. Some studies have indicated that HCWs had symptoms of mental illness (Jalloh et al., 2018; Li et al., 2015; Scott et al., 2009), and some studies have not found any mental health symptoms in this population (Khalid et al., 2016; Moll, 2014). This study was conducted in an attempt to delve deeper to address this contradiction. A qualitative inquiry involving in-depth exploration of HCWs' perceptions of their mental health while providing care for patients with EVD was conducted to add to the body of knowledge. The purpose of this study was to enable HCWs in Freetown, Sierra Leone to voice their opinions of the mental health symptoms they experienced while providing care for EVD clients.

Stress model theory guided this qualitative research study. While many studies have been conducted on the physical health of HCWs related to EVD (Coltart et al., 2015), limited literature exists on the mental health of HCWs treating patients with EVD. Research has provided insight on how many HCWs died (WHO, 2016) and how many contracted the virus during the EVD epidemic (CDC, 2015; WHO, 2016). Waldrop, Kramer, Skretny, Milch, and Finn (2005) used the stress process model theory in a qualitative study to interview 74 people who were providing hospice care for family members. They found that some of the stressors involved with family members were role conflict, work conflict, and financial strain.

In addition, Pack (2014) used the stress process model theory in a qualitative phenomenological study to interview 13 social workers. Participants in this study were asked how they would respond to a critical outbreak. This study found that preparation, positive relationships among peers, and support from management helped them during a catastrophic outbreak. There has been no study specifically addressing HCWs' perspectives on their mental health during the EVD outbreak. Thus, I sought to explore how HCWs in Freetown, Sierra Leone described their mental health symptoms, the stress they experienced, and the coping skills they used when treating patients with EVD.

This chapter includes are view of the literature on the research topic based on the research questions and the methodology. A literature review involves research synthesis and critical evaluation of existing literature related to the topic being studied (APA, 2000). The literature review identifies gaps in the literature. This literature review focuses on HCWs' perceptions of their mental health during the 2014 and 2015 Ebola outbreak because there had been limited research on the mental health aspect of HCWs' experiences during the EVD outbreak (CDC, 2015; WHO, 2016). This literature review covers key concepts related to phenomenological studies, EVD, mental health issues in West Africa, barriers to mental health care, stress factors related to mental health, coping skills, and epidemics.

Literature Search Strategy

Walden University provided me with relevant literature for this study. Search engines used to gather literature included the Sacramento Public Library, ProQuest Central, Academic Search, Google Academic, and the CDC website. I searched for relevant literature by using terms closely related to the current study. I chose the following as search terms: *stress process model, conceptual framework, phenomenology and healthcare workers, EVD, the healthcare system in Africa, inadequate mental healthcare and healthcare workers, HCWs and stress, HCWs and coping, barriers to mental health,* and *epidemic and healthcare workers.*

Theoretical Framework

Origin of the Stress Process Model

The stress process model was first introduced by Pearlin et al. in 1981 and was further developed by Pearlin in 1999. The stress process model, which was used as a theory in this study, asserts that three factors describe the stress process: stressors, moderators or mediators, and stressed outcomes (Pearlin et al., 1981). Stressors involve both internal and external factors. Internal factors involve individual biological and psychological factors that enable a person to confront a situation, whereas external factors involve the immediate individual environment or social context. Moderators or mediators involve the strengthening or weakening of specific elements based on the social or personal factors involved. According to Pearlin (1989, 1999), stress outcomes are the physiological and emotional effects on the person or persons involved. Pearlin postulated that there are two main categories of stressors: event stressors and chronic stressors. Event stressors are stressors that happen when a person does not expect the stress to occur. An example of an event stressor is an unexpected car crash on the way to work. The 2014 outbreak of the Ebola virus in West Africa was also categorized as an event stressor. Chronic stressors involve different kinds of strains (Pearlin& Skaff, 1996). Status, role, contextual, and quotidian strains are considered weak stressors. Unlike event stressors, chronic stressors include those resulting from a biased system that promotes inequality and injustice and exists for a period of time. These stressors persist despite being verbalized by the person or persons they affect.

Pearlin (1999) postulated that status strain involves an individual's social and hierarchical structure. In the context of HCWs during the EVD outbreak, an obvious example of this stressor is the lack of mental health funding in West Africa, which affects mental health services. This issue causes individuals in this population to be susceptible to an increased amount of stress. Pearlin stated that limitations on their personal and social resources cause HCWs to deal with stressors and increase their stress level. According to Pearlin, this can lead to longer-lasting and more profound stress.

Pearlin (1995) postulated that role strains are stressors comprising family roles, occupational roles, and institutional roles. An example of this type of stressor, as experienced by HCWs, is an increased demand of work beyond the job description.

Pearlin indicated that when a job is challenging and intertwined with abstract thinking skills, it creates stress for the employee, especially when it does not coincide with rewarding incentives. Pearlin's assessment of role strain suggests that the strain factors are intertwined with other stress factors.

The kind of strain that is most relevant to this study is Pearlin's (1999) concept of role conflict. Role conflict is relevant because individuals are exposed to stressors from various areas of their perceived roles. According to Pearlin, role conflict exposes an individual to stressors, which cause increased stress. Pearlin (1995) described the impact of gradual changes to family roles as an example of role conflict. For instance, most people depend on their family for both social and psychological support. Teenagers may feel role strain when their parents treat them like young children. As these teenagers become adults and their parents become unable to function independently, they develop the role strain of caring for their aging parents. According to Pearlin, constant realignment and restructuring are needed to cope with changing role settings. This role conflict also applies to HCWs who strive to provide care for both patients and family members, simultaneously fulfilling their responsibilities at work and home. The HCWs' roles as primary caregivers and support systems for their clients promote role conflict and thus cause them to experience high levels of psychological stress.

Contextual strains, according to Pearlin, involve strain between individuals and their environment, which consists of the community and the neighborhood. Pearlin (1995) provided an example by way of exploratory qualitative interviews in which participants in the study indicated that they experienced trepidation and uncertainty. This finding suggests that there were threats to the safety and security of the participants' well-being in their neighborhood. During the EVD outbreak, HCWs experienced both individual and environmental strains. Individual strains included the HCWs' psychological symptoms during the EVD outbreak, whereas environmental strains involved lack of resources and environmental support.

Finally, according to Pearlin, quotidian strains involve how individuals deal with their everyday lives. According to Pearlin, this kind of strain comes from normal activities both within and outside the home. For instance, doing laundry on a regular basis cannot be avoided if one wants to wear clean clothes. However, for some individuals, this task causes stress and strain. Another example is going to bed on time to have a productive next day. For some people, this quotidian activity causes strain. An example of quotidian strain could be HCWs experiencing long hours of work and being unable to get a restful night's sleep. Given the compelling evidence that many caregivers have experienced psychological stress(Jalloh et al., 2018; Li et al., 2015; Scott et al., 2009), they should have access to quality mental health care to help them cope with psychological stress. I designed this study to explore the perceptions of HCWs concerning their mental health while providing care for patients with EVD.

Rationale for the Theoretical Framework

Pearlin employed this theoretical framework to argue that individuals are connected to social structures that influence their lives. The social structures of HCWs who have cared for EVD patients relate to the roles of their employers, the government, and other social factors that force them to be exposed to certain events. In this study, I focused on HCWs' connections to the social structure of a hospital or clinic that provided care for Ebola virus patients. Though HCWs' hard work and extraordinary time spent with clients during the epidemic saved many lives, international organizations also played a considerable role in helping to provide support during the Ebola outbreak (CDC, 2015; WHO, 2016). According to Pearlin (1999), the stress process model can be used in the medical field to examine the health and well-being of those who care for persons with health problems and disabilities. I decided that this model would be optimal for this study because of the role that HCWs played in treating patients with EVD during the 2014 outbreak. The HCWs certainly influenced the patients, but the patients also influenced the HCWs. The stress process model was selected over other potential models because it facilitated this study's analysis of relevant information about HCWs' perspectives on the stress they experienced while providing care for patients with EVD in Freetown, Sierra Leone.

A theory is able to explain why behaviors occur (Creswell, 2009). This theory was selected because it relates to the roles that HCWs play in their everyday lives. The stress process model was applicable to the analysis of what the HCWs said about the mental health symptoms that they experienced while providing care for Ebola virus patients. The stress process model was the most appropriate model for this study (Pearlin, 1989, 1991). The research questions were derived from the premise of the stress process model. This study was built on this existing theory as it helped to explain and identify views of HCWs in Freetown, Sierra Leone on how they coped with the stress factors and their own mental health when treating patients with EVD. This theory brought light to the understanding of how different stressors can cause mental illness.

Conceptual Framework

Phenomenology formed the conceptual framework for this study. Heidegger (1889) used a conceptual framework of hermeneutic phenomenology to understand lived experiences of different phenomena. Like many conceptual frameworks, hermeneutic phenomenology can be used to understand HCWs' perspectives on their mental health during the 2014 and 2015 EVD outbreak. van Manen (2014) used hermeneutic phenomenology to purport that individuals have different ways of experiencing different phenomena. The social situation that HCWs experienced could include the healthcare system, government regulations or funding, and their patients. This study focused on HCWs who were involved with the social structure of clinics and hospitals during the 2014 to 2015 EVD outbreak in Freetown, Sierra Leone.

The hermeneutic phenomenological conceptual framework is widely used by individuals to explain their ways of seeing things, knowing things, and understanding how things relate to them (Valandra, 2012). More specifically, it provides a framework for understanding the mental health symptoms that HCWs experienced while providing care for patients during the EVD outbreak of 2014 to 2015. Researchers applying Heidegger's concept of hermeneutic phenomenology employ intuition, reduction, and intersubjectivity to understand the meaning of phenomena (Patton, 2002). In using

Heidegger's conceptual framework of hermeneutic phenomenology in this study, I sought to understand HCWs' perspectives on their mental health during the EVD outbreak in Freetown, Sierra Leone.

Literature Review Related to Key Concepts

This literature review provides an overview of HCWs' perceptions of their mental health when working with highly infectious patients. Qualitative, phenomenology, and quantitative studies were chosen methodology and methods that set the foundation for this study. The studies cited in the subsections that follow are related to the construct of interest and the chosen methodology and are consistent with the scope of the study.

Phenomenology

According to Brinkmann (2014) and Converse (2012), phenomenology is a philosophy and are search strategy that is used to understand individuals' perceptions of their lived experiences. An area of phenomenology is hermeneutic phenomenology. Originating in Husserl's work, hermeneutic phenomenology was founded by Heidegger (1889), a student of Husserl (Converse, 2012). As Pietkiewicz and Smith (2014) stated, phenomenology is the study of human lived experiences, and the key elements of phenomenology are description, reduction, essence, and intentionality. In the reduction process, Patton (2002) indicated that the researcher's goal is to describe the individual's personal experience of the phenomenon of interest without influencing the outcome of the result. When the individual expresses his or her feelings about his or her lived experiences, this process is called an *essence*. Intentionality, according to Converse (2012) and Peredaryenko and Krauss (2013), involves the ability of individuals to describe what things mean to them. According to Tuohy et al. (2013) and Valandra (2012), hermeneutic phenomenology is one of the components of phenomenology. I selected hermeneutic phenomenology because of its descriptive and interpretive components. The application of hermeneutic phenomenology in this study included the use of semi structured interviews to communicate with participants.

Phenomenological Studies of Healthcare Workers

Jonsson and Halabi (2006) conducted a phenomenological study on the consequences of work-related stress among HCWs in the Middle East. Their study aimed to understand the relationship between stress exposure and posttraumatic stress disorder. They interviewed 25 nurses. They found that stress-related symptoms are related to poor social support. They also found that HCWs in the Middle East were at serious risk for a high level of stress symptoms. They concluded that their study would enable HCWs to deal with stress in an early efficient manner.

Corley, Hammond, and Fraser (2010) conducted a phenomenological study on the lived experiences of HCWs working in the intensive care unit during the H1N1 influenza pandemic in Australia. They found that eight common themes emerge from the study. Some of the themes are (a) the wearing of protective equipment, (a) infection control procedure, and (c) morale level. They concluded this study indicated that the planning for an epidemic is stressful because of its unpredictable nature.

Troy, Wyness, and McAuliffe (2007) conducted a qualitative study on HCWs using a phenomenological approach. They interviewed 12 HCWs in South Africa and the Philippines. They found that there was a high turnover among HCWs and it was challenging to recruit HCWs because of language and cultural differences.

Matiti (2005) used a phenomenology approach to study the cultural experiences of internationally recruited nurses. Matiti interviewed 12 nurses—seven females and five males. Matiti found that cultural perception of nurses influences their adaptation at their workplace.

In another study, Gustafsson, Norberg, and Strandberg (2008) interviewed 20 female healthcare professionals. They used a phenomenological approach to ask healthcare workers about burnout at work. They found that healthcare workers who are autonomous in their jobs can avoid burnout. However, healthcare workers that were dissatisfied at their jobs were prone to burnout.

Ebola Virus Disease

According to Beeching, Fenech, and Houlihan (2014), there are three phases of symptoms associated with the Ebola virus disease. The first phase of symptoms includes fever, headache, and myalgia. The second phase of symptoms is gastrointestinal, such as diarrhea and vomiting. The third phase of symptoms includes loss of consciousness and bleeding. According to the WHO (2014) the most common symptoms reported during the 2014 Sierra Leone EVD outbreak were: "Fever (87.1%), fatigue (76.4%), loss of appetite (64.5%), vomiting (67.6%), diarrhea (65.6%), headache (53.4%), abdominal pain (44.3%), and unexplained bleeding (18%)" (p. 3). Researchers indicated that children and adults exhibit similar symptoms. However, younger children exhibit more respiratory difficulties as compared to adults (CDC, 2014). Patient's temperature, blood pressure, pulse rate, and respiration should be monitored after an EVD diagnosis (Beeching et al., 2014). Other possible symptoms related to the EVD are maculopapular rash, bleeding, hepatomegaly, lymphadenopathy, and geological signs (CDC, 2014). However, early recognition of the first two phases of symptoms and diagnosis of the EVD can help save the lives of patients and healthcare workers.

Symptoms and Diagnosis of EVD

The EVD is diagnosed by the collection of specimens, a process that is under strict precaution guidelines (Beeching et al., 2014). A patient is diagnosed after a test shows positive Ebola RT-PCR (CDC, 2014). When a patient or HCW is isolated because of a suspected case of the EVD, this test is ordered. A positive test indicates that the patient or HCW is infected with the EVD. Usually, a negative test is repeated within 48 hours after the first test to confirm the result (Beeching et al., 2014). The EVD is best managed by early diagnosis and supportive treatment (CDC, 2014). Beeching et al. (2014) have suggested that high fatality rates in emerging countries occur because of a lack of proper funding for basic health care. Beeching et al. and the CDC also indicated that the EVD could be easily misdiagnosed as malaria because of the increased temperature of the patient. However, if the patient continues to exhibit symptoms of uncontrolled diarrhea and vomiting, they are at risk of the EVD. Because of the lack of funding, patients with malaria are often misdiagnosed with the EVD. This creates a stressful situation for HCWs because it causes confusion regarding diagnosis and treatment.

Management, Treatment, and Prognosis

There have been over 26,277 confirmed cases of Ebola in Sierra Leone, Guinea, and Liberia (Beavogui et al., 2016). There were 10,884 EVD related deaths between December of 2013 and April of 2015 (WHO, 2015). The CDC has suggested that a patient who is suspected to have the EVD must be isolated from the public and should be monitored for the duration of the incubation. HCWs suspected to have the EVD should be treated the same way as other suspected patients. The CDC indicated that HCWs who are exposed to body fluid from a patient should wash affected areas with soap and copious amount of water. There is no known cure for the EVD; the treatments currently available are fluid for hydration and anti-nausea medication (Saxena & Gomes, 2016). The fluid provides electrolyte replacement, which decreases the mortality rates in some patients with the EVD (WHO, 2014). Beeching et al. (2014) addressed the steps of symptomatic management for the EVD that are recommended by healthcare providers. Fever and pain are to be treated with paracetamol and morphine for severe pain. Non- steroid medications are to be avoided because of excessive bleeding. Nausea and vomiting are to be treated with intravenous anti-emetics, and omeprazole is recommended for heartburn. Benzodiazepines are recommended when the patient is experiencing seizures. Though seizures are uncommon, HCWs should be prepared to treat them. Phenobarbital is given if the patient is exhibiting repeated seizures. Haldol or benzodiazepine are used if the patient is agitated. HCWs should be prepared to avoid body contact to minimize risk of needlestick injuries. The best-known treatment for the EVD is the ZMapp. Research has suggested that the ZMapp is a combination of three EV "glycoprotein epitopes and it's engineered for expression in tobacco plants" (Beeching et al., 2014, p. 7). ZMapp had been proven to be effective when given to nonhuman primates; however, it has not yet been successfully tested in humans. Beeching et al. also indicated that the drug Favipiravir was proven to be effective in treating the influenza virus, West Nile virus, and yellow fever. It has proven to be effective in treating the EVD in mice. However, it has not yet been proven to be effective in human subjects. These studies indicate that the EVD is deadly and there is no available cure, which causes stress among healthcare workers. However, following safety measures and using effective coping skills can help HCWs deal with this deadly virus (Khalid et al., 2016).

There is a higher mortality rate for the EVD among children under the age of five and adults over the age of 40 (CDC, 2014). The CDC reported that pregnant women have a higher chance of miscarriage after being diagnosed with the Ebola virus disease. However, early diagnosis helps promote the survival of the virus.

The management, treatment, and prognosis of the EVD are relevant to this study. However, how HCWs describe their mental health symptoms while working with infectious patients in a poor-quality healthcare system applies to this study. Reviewing additional literature that provides information on the healthcare system in West Africa is addressed in the next paragraph.

History of Healthcare for Mental Illness in West Africa

In the 1800s, African men from the Yoruba tribe from Sierra Leone, West Africa left their native land to study medicine in the United Kingdom (Oyebode, 2006). Oyebode stated that during the colonial times, most the men who went to study medicine in the United Kingdom returned as medical doctors. In the 1800s, the African government began formulating plans to help the mentally ill in colonial Africa (Oyebode, 2006). However, psychiatry, related to mental health in Africa did not start until the 1900s. Oyebode postulated in the 1900s, African medical doctors were encouraged by the government to practice psychiatry in West Africa. Forster (2012) cited that before 1951 there was no African psychiatrist in colonial Africa. Forster indicated after 1951 there were just four psychiatrists in the entire continent of Africa.

The first mental health hospitals in West Africa were in Nigeria, Ghana, and Sierra Leone (Manuwa, 1971). During the 1900s African patients were treated separately from European patients in these mental health hospitals and African doctors were paid less than European doctors (Oyebode, 2006). Similarly, Schram (1971) has suggested that racial origin played a significant role in psychiatry in West Africa. Oyebode postulated that the government was looking for a way to build a hospital that would treat patients with the principles of fairness, respect, and compassion. In 1957 the Kissy Lunatic Asylum in Freetown, Sierra Leone started treating patients with mental illness. Many of the asylums were considered prison cells for convicted felons, such as the Kissy Lunatic Asylum that was built in 1847(Sadowsky, 1999). Sadowsky reported that the asylums were not properly kept, lacked basic supplies, were dark and congested, and patients were shackled. McCulloch (1995) noted that most of the mentally ill people in West Africa were treated like convicted felons as compared to mentally ill patients in the developed world. For instance, patients were kept in small cells in their own feces and urine.

The African population was reluctant to accept psychiatry during the colonial days. Csordas and Lewton (1998) indicated that Africans during colonialism believed that psychiatry was witchcraft, juju, taboos, and a religious cult. Sadowsky also emphasized the fact that some of the people who were diagnosed as mentally ill were people who stood up against colonization. Forster (2012) noted that the cultural conditioning of Africans toward psychiatry prevents many Africans to go into the field of psychiatry. Forster added that some Sierra Leoneans believed that psychiatric patients were religiously possessed as they were punished for their sins. In 1900, Forster stated that it was a challenging time for psychiatry in Africa as compared to the current psychiatry.

McCulloch (1995) postulated that colonialization influenced modern psychiatry in West Africa. In other words, all the psychological concepts used in African psychiatry came from white society. For instance, African society was described as sexually promiscuous, violent, lazy, and savagery. According to McCulloch, "ethnopsychiatry was the settlers' most eloquent response to the challenge of African nationalism" (p. 334).

Forster (2012) pointed out that more African doctors from Africa are studying psychiatry in the United Kingdom, Canada, and other parts of the world today as compared to the colonial days. Forster added that the attitude of the population toward psychiatry has changed as many Africans have embraced psychiatry to understand the meaning of mental illness. Forster included that there are many Africans seeking psychiatric help as compared to none in the colonial days. Forster added that despite the beliefs of psychiatry in Africa by some Africans, some Africans still hold on to their cultural beliefs after they are discharged from the hospital. Forster indicated that one of the current problems facing psychiatry in West Africa is the overcrowding of patients in clinics. The overcrowding is caused by limited mental institutions. The current psychiatric treatment in Africa is pharmacotherapy and psychotherapy (Forster, 2012).

Forster indicated that patients are admitted voluntarily, and the extent of mental illness in West Africa is unknown as many patients are misdiagnosed. Forster indicated that there are no special laws for defective individuals with mental problems. The sample of the study was collected in Ghana, West Africa. According to Forster, many of the patients in Ghana have schizophrenia. Forster cited that the need for psychiatrists is in great demand in the continent of Africa.

Sukeri, Betancourt, and Emsley (2014) postulated that mental health service in Africa is mixed with colonial history and apartheid. Sukeri, Betancourt, and Emsley indicated that, before the development of formalized mental health services, mental health care was provided through a network of public assistance and missionary hospitals. Sukeri, Betancourt, and Emsley noted that the historical context of mental health in Africa affects the current status of psychiatry in Africa. The WHO (2014) indicated that funding for mental health clinics in the West African region remains low, while funding for mental illness in developed nations remains high. Therefore, because of the historical context, lack of funding for mental health clinics, lack of knowledge, and stigmatization, Africans are often afraid to be labeled mentally ill.

Healthcare System in West Africa

In addition, poor quality healthcare system can affect the role of healthcare workers. Brolin Ribacke et al. (2016) reported that during the Ebola crisis of 2014 in West Africa, Sierra Leone, the healthcare system was deplorable. They indicated because of the inadequate health care system in Sierra Leone, HCWs were afraid to go to work. Brolin Ribacke et al. postulated that one of the problems associated with the healthcare system in Sierra Leone is the lack of incentives for healthcare workers. Many HCWs in Sierra Leone prefer to work for an NGO organization for better salary than for the government of Sierra Leone. They found that the main hospital in Freetown, Sierra Leone called Connaught lacks the necessary medical supplies such as sterilized needles, proper clothing for an epidemic, and catheters for patients that need them (Greenberg et al., 2015). Brolin Ribacke et al. stated that healthcare assistance is inadequate because the government failed to provide basic resources to healthcare workers. For instance, poor transportation and the lack of infrastructure make it difficult for many HCWs, especially those that are poor. Healthcare workers are underpaid and showed no motivation to perform their duties.

Parpia, Ndeffo-Mbah, Wenzel, and Galvani (2016) examined the effect of the response of the 2014 to 2015 EVD outbreak in West Africa. They conducted a three- computational simulation on the healthcare system in Sierra Leone, Liberia, and Guinea. A quantitative study was performed using a survey to gather the data from participants. They indicated that the Ebola outbreak of 2014 and 2015 affected the healthcare system, the diagnosis of malaria, HIV/AIDS, and tuberculosis. They argued that the deaths of several HCWs and the limited number of HCWs affected the healthcare system. According to their findings, they indicated that fear of transmission of the EVD was another factor that affected the healthcare system and healthcare workers. Also, mandatory emergency curfew, border closures, and transportation difficulties all affected the healthcare system and healthcare workers.

Ansumana et al. (2017) cited that the Mano River Union (MRU) was found to help the healthcare system in West Africa so that HCWs can provide effective care for their patients. According to Ansumana et al., the healthcare assistance in the MRU countries includes a prevention program for tuberculosis. Ansumana et al. indicated that during the outbreak of the EVD, most of the HCWs contracted the virus and eventually died. According to Ansumana et al., there were 810 confirmed deaths among HCWs in Sierra Leone, Liberia, and Guinea.

Fasina et al. (2015) cited that the healthcare system during the EVD outbreak in 2014 was deplorable. They conducted a qualitative study in West Africa during the EVD outbreak of 2014. They found that the reason for the increase in death was based on the poor healthcare system. Their findings suggest the need for a quality healthcare system in West Africa in case there is another outbreak of the EVD

The healthcare system has been a challenge for HCWs since and after the EVD outbreak of 2014 in Sierra Leone (Alonso et al., 2014). Some of the challenges of the healthcare system are (a) lack of proper health infrastructure, (b) the lack of appropriate treatment method to control the spread of the Ebola virus disease, and (c) the lack of trust of healthcare workers by the population. Healthcare workers in Sierra Leone ranked the EVD as a serious problem in West Africa (Wenshu et al., 2014). They indicated that understanding the factors contributing to the problems of the healthcare system would help promote adequate health care system in Sierra Leone.

Healthcare Workers and Mental Health

Psychological problems for healthcare workers are a growing concern, especially in the West African region. Mugisha et al. (2017) indicated that there would be an increase in mental health problems among HCWs in West Africa if better strategies for adequate mental healthcare are not implemented. Abendroth and Flannery (2006) indicated because HCWs provide a high degree of quality care for their patients, they suffer from compassion fatigue (CF). According to Abendroth and Flannery, CF can cause physical and psychological problems for healthcare workers. It is reasonable to argue that good mental health enables HCWs to provide effective care to their clients. Betancourt et al. (2016) and CDC (2015) have confirmed that if adequate resources are not provided to HCWs in West Africa, it will be difficult for them to provide adequate treatment to their patients.

Khalid et al. (2016) found that HCWs in Saudi Arabia contracted the Middle East respiratory syndrome coronavirus (MERS-COV) while providing care for their patients. They exhibited the symptoms of diarrhea, difficulty breathing, nausea, and vomiting. The fatality rate among HCWs during the MERS-COV outbreak was between 30%

and 70%. The overall fatality rate was 35%, and the mortality rate among ventilated patients was 60% to 70%. HCWs who experienced MERS-Cov experienced significant stress and emotional problems. HCWs remained emotionally committed to their jobs during the MERS-COV outbreak despite the deaths of some of their co-workers. Moll (2014) postulated that HCWs are committed to their work despite their high rates of stress. Moll found that HCWs with mental health issues are ostracized by society and suggested that, if adequate care is not provided, their symptoms might get worse. He indicated that poor mental health among HCWs affects not only their families but also their patients and society. Therefore, because HCWs are emotionally committed to their work, they need effective strategies to cope with the stress factors they experience.

Mental health problems can affect the quality of services provided by healthcare workers. Koinis et al. (2015) postulated that workplace stress influences the physical and emotional well-being of healthcare workers. In their quantitative study, Koinis et al. (2015) sampled 200 HCWs to identify their coping strategies at work. The results indicated that most HCWs do not have stress management techniques. They recommended stress management technique for healthcare workers. If the psychological problems among HCWs are not taken seriously in the West African nations, HCWs will have difficulties providing quality care to their clients. Some of the emotional problems HCWs experience include anxiety, depression, and PTSD (Li et al., 2015; Shoji et al., 2014). These emotional difficulties can cause HCWs to abuse drugs and alcohol to cope with their psychological problems (Charlson, Diminic, Lund, Degenhardt, &Whiteford, 2014). Mateen and Dorji (2009) found that HCWs who exhibit mental difficulties are at a greater risk for suicide. There is no clinic in Sierra Leone that provides adequate mental health treatment for healthcare workers (Alonso et al., 2014). HCWs with undiagnosed mental health issues are likely to have difficulties adjusting to their everyday lives (WHO, 2016). The WHO (2016) has indicated that mental health disorders among HCWs, especially HCWs combating outbreaks and epidemics, are likely to impact their lives both psychologically and physiologically. Therefore, numerous studies have contended that HCWs experience high levels of stress and that a lack of stress management techniques may affect the quality of their work performance.

Shoji et al. (2014) studied the increase in PTSD among healthcare workers. In their quantitative study, they found that direct exposure to a traumatic event is related to posttraumatic stress disorder (PTSD). They conducted two studies of a total of 408 participants working in behavioral healthcare in the U.S. They found that some of the symptoms of PTSD include re-experiencing, avoidance, and hyperarousal. Bride, Robinson, Yegidis, and Figley (2004) postulated that secondary traumatic stress (STS) is an indirect exposure to a traumatic situation. STS is commonly seen among HCWs who are providing care for traumatized patients. These studies indicate that PTSD and STS occur among HCWs who are exposed to outbreaks or an epidemic. Higher levels of distress and negative cognition are experienced by HCWs who are exposed to these negative situations (Shoji et al., 2014).

Ansumana et al. (2017) stated that HCWs in Sierra Leone during the EVD outbreak experienced low self-esteem, lack of trust toward the healthcare system, and a feeling of loneliness. They found that HCWs were restricted to attend the burial of their loved ones and to touch their families or colleagues. These restrictions left them feeling lonely and isolated. However, this study did not cover the mental health of HCWs while providing care for the EVD patients, an area that was explored in this study.

Analysis of Healthcare Workers and Mental Health

The studies addressed above indicated that the mental healthcare of HCWs cannot be ignored, especially in an epidemic. Mugisha et al. (2017), Abendroth and Flannery (2006), Khalid et al. (2016), and Moll (2014) all suggested that poor mental health is a significant risk among healthcare workers. Mugisha et al. found increased mental illness among HCWs, while Abendroth and Flannery identified compassion fatigue among HCWs as a mental health concern. Koinis et al. (2015) found that most HCWs did not have stress management techniques.

Mateen and Dorji (2009) found that HCWs have a high risk of suicide. Shoji et al. (2014) found that posttraumatic stress disorder and secondary traumatic stress are found among HCWs who are exposed to an epidemic. These studies recommended that additional measures should be taken to help HCWs cope with mental illness. However, asking HCWs how they cope with their mental health when working with infectious patients during the EVD is relevant to the study. This was the area that was explored in this study.

Further, Li et al. (2015) found that anxiety and depression are the two most common mental health problems among healthcare workers. However, these researchers did not explicitly elaborate on the extent of these mental health symptoms of healthcare workers. The WHO (2016) has called for immediate attention regarding the mental health crisis in Africa. Numerous studies have therefore recommended that additional measures be taken to help address the mental health crisis among HCWs in Africa. These studies together confirmed that HCWs might experience mental health issues, especially in a traumatic situation.

Based on the quantitative pieces of literature, HCWs have been found to exhibit mental health symptoms such as anxiety, PTSD, and depression (Gwaikolo et al., 2017; Li et al., 2015; Shoji et al., 2014). While the qualitative studies show that HCWs experience GF, lack of adequate resources, low self-esteem, and high stress (Abendroth & Flannery, 2006; Ansumana et al., 2017; CDC, 2015; Khalid et al., 2016; Moll, 2014). Therefore, the extent of mental health issues among HCWs treating patients with the EVD is unknown, and the findings are mixed. Thus, the advantage of doing a qualitative study over quantitative study was that a qualitative study enabled me to get an in-depth understanding of the perspectives of HCWs regarding any mental health issues they experienced and the care they received. This study explored HCWs perspectives on how they cope with stress while providing care for patients with the Ebola virus disease. This study would encourage mental healthcare providers, as well as policymakers to incorporate effective measures to address the mental health crisis in Africa.

Mental Health Treatment and Cost

Padayacheya, Ramlalla, and Chipps (2017) employed a quantitative research method to study depression in older adults by assessing the cost associated with their mental health treatment in South Africa. They found that the cost of mental health treatment, especially for depression, is lower when it is diagnosed early. To determine the prevalence of depression among South Africans, they used a 15-item genetic depression scale. They also used a sociodemographic questionnaire on 255 geriatric patients. The data were compared to other mental health care systems in Africa. They concluded that early diagnosis of mental illness cost less as compared to late diagnosis when dealing with mental illness in South Africa.

Musa et al. (2016) used a quantitative research method to evaluate cost optimization in the treatment of multi-drug-resistant tuberculosis (MDR TB) in Nigeria, West Africa and determined the cost differences between home-based treatment and hospital treatment. They found that patients who were treated for MDR TB at home saved 35% as compared to patients who were treated in a hospital setting. The study found that the associated costs for a hospital stay were very expensive. The treatment costs for patients with family support were lower. However, one major limitation associated with the study was that the researchers did not provide any information on psychotropic medications related to mental illness. The researchers recommended further studies on public costs related to health care in Africa.

Lund et al. (2013) studied mental illness and lost income among 4,351 adults in South Africa and found that anxiety and depression can prevent South Africans from obtaining affordable living and mental health care. The study found that mental illness is a major economic disadvantage for the low-income population in Africa. Individuals in lower income groups were unable to obtain adequate mental health services. Lund et al. (2013) also found that the mental health cost for adults in South Africa is estimated at $59 million annually. They also evaluated both the direct and indirect costs of mental health care in Africa and found that the indirect cost outweighs the direct cost. They suggested that indirect cost means the cost of lost income based on unexpected unemployment and recommended government assistance to help cover indirect costs for low-income individuals.

In a similar quantitative study, Lund, Boyce, Flisher, Kafaar, and Dawes (2009) studied human resource requirements and cost for mental health care among children and adolescents in South Africa. They found that children and adolescents pay a total of $5.99 to $21.50 per hospital visit. They indicated that this cost model could be used in other parts of Africa for mental health services and made recommendations for better calculation of low-cost mental health care in low and middle-income countries. Flisher et al. (1997) found that both direct and indirect costs for mental health services in South Africa were affected by apartheid. They stated that the public policy of apartheid did not provide adequate mental healthcare for ethnic Africans. However, after the apartheid government, mental health care did include ethnic Africans with mental illness.

deMenil et al. (2014) indicated that there is a wide margin between the need and treatment for mental disorders in Africa. The researchers used a quantitative method to study a 30-bed psychiatric hospital in Nairobi Kenya, in Africa. They indicated that mental health cost is mostly funded by a private insurance company (PHI). They evaluated the effect of PHI in the largest private psychiatric hospital in East Africa. The study utilized a Multilinear and binary logistic regression to examine the impact of PHI related to the admission, readmission, and the length of stay of patients in the hospital. They indicated that 66.4% of patients were male and they were voluntarily admitted to the hospital. However, 70% of the patients were involuntarily admitted to the hospital.

According to this study, 31.6% of the patients were diagnosed with substance abuse and that 1.6% were diagnosed with serious mental health problems. They indicated that two-thirds of the patients received individual counseling and group therapy. And most of the patients were prescribed psychotropic medications. The study found that patients with PHI received better treatment than patients who paid out of their pockets. Also, patients that paid out of their pocket had 2.5% odds of relapsing within 12 months after being discharged. The study also found that PHI was billed at a 7.1% more than patients who paid out of their pockets. They concluded that the cost for mental health is Kenya benefits only individuals with private health insurance.

Evans-Lacko and Knapp (2016) utilized a quantitative method on the cost of depression across eight diverse countries. The researchers reviewed data collected in the Global Impact of Depression in the Workplace in Europe Audit. The data was collected from employees that were absent from work due to depression. The researchers reviewed focused on the cost of depression from South Africa, Brazil, China, Canada, Korea, Japan, and Mexico. They indicated that the economic cost of depression is affecting employers' work productivity. The study found that there is a high financial cost for employers in South Africa than the other countries studied.

The above-reviewed literature addressed the costs related to mental illness in Africa. Lund et al. (2013) indicated that mental health cost in Africa is difficult among South Africans that are unemployed. Lund et al. (2009) found that children and adolescents paid the same for mental health cost in South Africa. deMenil et al. (2014) provided relevant information related to PHI in East Africa. Evans-Lacko and Knapp (2016) provided relevant information on the cost employers pay for mental healthcare for their employees in South Africa. Musa et al. (2016) provided information about the cost of a hospital stay and homestay in West Africa. These studies confirmed that effective cost strategies for mental health are needed to promote efficient mental health service in Africa. These studies also confirmed that the cost of mental healthcare in Africa was inadequate, as this could promote stress for HCWs. Therefore, the question is- How do HCWs cope with inadequate mental healthcare while providing treatments to the Ebola virus patients in Freetown, Sierra Leoneans? Reviewing additional pieces of literature that provide information on the inadequate mental healthcare and HCWs are addressed in the next paragraph.

Inadequate Mental Healthcare and Healthcare Workers

Inadequate mental healthcare programs affect the psychological well-being of healthcare workers. Khalid et al. (2016) have argued that every disease outbreak is unique in its totality, geographical location, pathogenesis, transmissibility, and effectivity. HCWs in the Western region of Africa experienced psychological stress because of inadequate mental healthcare and poor living conditions (CDC, 2015; WHO, 2016). While developed nations receive adequate mental healthcare treatment for psychological problems, West African nation's mental healthcare treatment is inadequate to help HCWs with psychological problems, especially during an epidemic (Betancourt et al., 2016; WHO, 2016). The government is the primary influence on HCWs' psychological well-being in Sierra Leone, and several studies have called for adequate mental health care for HCWs in the West African region (Betancourt et al., 2016; WHO, 2016). The above studies showed inadequate or nonexistence mental healthcare for HCWs promotes psychological stress (Betancourt et al., 2016; CDC, 2015;

WHO, 2016). HCWs take risks to help their patients without access to quality psychological care for themselves. Khalid et al. (2016) noted that HCWs often have emotional problems and require mental health care. In Sierra Leone, mental illness among HCWs is not diagnosed as quickly as that of HCWs in developed nations because of the lack of adequate resources (CDC, 2015; Greenberg et al., 2015). These findings give credence to Greenberg et al.'s claim that inadequate resources for mental health care in Africa are preventing early diagnosis. The number of HCWs with mental illness in Sierra Leone should be investigated to prove the need for mental health services that would help them cope with stress during the next outbreak or epidemic.

Clinics and hospitals can enhance the work of HCWs by providing them with quality psychological and physiological care. Even though clinics and hospitals are designed to provide adequate care for patients, poor mental health among HCWs affects the quality of their work (Greenberg et al., 2015). Most of the clinics and hospitals in Sierra Leone are poorly funded by the government and rely primarily on international sponsors (Greenberg et al., 2015). Khalid et al. (2016) found that positive attitude and humor among colleagues in the workplace environment reduce stress. Also, HCWs who were provided adequate mental healthcare at their worksites reported a reduction in their psychological symptoms (deMenil et al., 2014; Li et al., 2015). HCWs are forced to work overtime during an outbreak or epidemic (Khalid et al., 2016). Khalid et al. also indicated, despite the emotional difficulties HCWs experienced, they were obligated to their ethical and professional duties in their work settings. Therefore, hospitals should focus on providing quality psychological help for healthcare workers. It is evident that providing adequate mental healthcare and emotional support will improve the psychological well-being of healthcare workers. These studies recommended that additional measures be taken to provide adequate mental healthcare for HCWs in Africa. Therefore, asking HCWs how they cope with their mental health when working with infectious patients during the EVD in an inadequate mental health setting was relevant to this study. This was the area that was explored in this study. Reviewing additional literature that provides information on HCWs and stress was significant for this study. As a result, literature addressing HCWs and stress is addressed in the next paragraph.

Healthcare Workers and Stress

Raab et al. (2015) conducted a study in Canada to determine the effectiveness of mindfulness-based stress reduction (MBSR) for treating healthcare workers. Glasberg et al. (2007) postulated that stress affects healthcare workers' work performance. This study was conducted at a large Canadian mental health center in an urban setting. Twenty-two female HCWs between the ages of 24 and 69 years were included in the study. Pre-and post-assessment measures consisted of the SCS, MBI, and QLI. They found that HCWs are vulnerable to stress overload and burnout (Harris, 2001; Moore & Cooper, 1996). They also found that HCWs experienced increased anxiety, depression, and mental fatigue (Myers, 1994; Radeke & Mahoney, 2000). However, they concluded that MBSR is an effective intervention to help HCWs cope with stress.

Shoji et al. (2014) conducted a quantitative study in the United States to determine traumatic growth among healthcare workers. Shoji et al. postulated that negative exposure to traumatic events causes psychological disorders such as posttraumatic stress disorder (PTSD). The study indicated that symptoms of PTSD include re-experiencing, avoidance, and hyperarousal (Brewin, Andrews, & Valentine, 2000). They indicated that secondary traumatic stress (STS) is indirect exposure to stress. The study found that individuals with STS exhibit the same symptoms as PTSD.

Pearlman and Mac Ian (1995) also noted that negative consequences and work distress affect HCWs' performance. They conducted two studies at a behavioral center in the United States. The first study involved 408 HCWs in the U.S. and the second study involved 487 HCWs from different backgrounds. HCWs in the first study were given questionnaires to rate their STS, perceived social support, and workplace burnout. HCWs in the second study were given the same questionnaire, with the inclusion of the SPS scale, STSE scale, MSPSS scale, and Posttraumatic Growth Inventory-Short Form. In both studies, the researchers found that the relationship between STS and STG was mediated by STSE and social support. The study concluded that education and social development programs would enable HCWs to boost their self-efficacy and perceived social support.

Ding, Qu, Yu, and Wang (2014) conducted a study in China to explore the relationship between occupational stress and anxiety symptoms among healthcare workers. They indicated that there are several occupational stressors that affect the quality of work HCWs provide to their clients. Ding et al. stated that one of the symptoms associated with HCWs' stress is anxiety. They conducted a cross-sectional survey of 1,752 HCWs, using questionnaires—the Zung Self Rating Anxiety Scale, the Chinese Fashion of the Effort-Reward Imbalance Scale, and the Maslach Burnout Inventory-General Survey—to rate anxiety symptoms. Additionally, they performed a hierarchical linear regression to assess the burnout effect of healthcare workers. The study found that the prevalence of anxiety symptoms among community HCWs was 38%. Thus, there is a relationship between burnout, occupational stress, and anxiety symptoms. They concluded that burnout mediates the effect of occupational stress and anxiety symptoms. Ding et al. recommended burnout management classes for HCWs to reduce the impact of occupational stress and anxiety symptoms.

In a qualitative study not related to the EVD, Scott et al. (2009) indicated that HCWs are second victims, especially when they watch their clients die. The researchers used a semi structured interview to ask HCWs if they experienced stress related to work problems that led to anxiety and depression. The key finding from this study was that HCWs "suffer alone" and they recommended that effective strategies should be implemented to help HCWs cope with stress related to their jobs (pg. 331).

Selamu et al. (2017) conducted a study in Ethiopia, Africa to explore the lived experiences of HCWs well-being, stress, and burnout when treating their patients. They postulated that HCWs' well-being is important so that they can provide quality care for their patients. This study was conducted in a primary healthcare setting in rural Ethiopia through in-depth interviews with 52 primary HCWs: 35 facility-based healthcare professionals and 17 community-based healthcare workers. The study found that facility- based HCWs think of well-being as the absence of stress. Participants indicated that the cause of their main stressors was inadequate medical supplies and the limited supplies might cause infection. They also indicated that performance evaluation in their work setting also provoked stress. In the community-based setting, HCWs reported role ambiguity to be their main stressor. Additionally, the study found that both groups suffered from heavy workloads and economic self-sufficiency. HCWs reported symptoms of burnout and emotional difficulties. Selamu et al. (2017) concluded that HCWs in Ethiopia are experiencing job-related stress that promotes burnout. They further indicated that job-related stress and burnout among HCWs created a high turnover of staff. They recommended a better understanding of job-related stress and burnout among HCWs to benefit healthcare professionals. However, this study did not address HCWs perspectives of their mental health during an epidemic, an area that was explored in this study.

Darboe, I-Feng, Hsien-Wen, Lin, and Kuo (2016) conducted a quantitative study in Gambia, West Africa to investigate perceived stress among healthcare workers. They postulated that the work of HCWs is critical to the community and suggested that HCWs should be free from inborn worries and anxieties. The study was conducted at the secondary public health facility in the Gambia and analyzed results from a cross-sectional random sample of 287 HCWs using a 22-item ERI. They used a single measure to assess perceived stress and subjective health among healthcare workers. They found that there was a relationship between perceived work stress and subjective health. They also found that high effort-reward imbalance is related to poor subjective health among HCWs in the Gambia. Psychosocial stress increases overall stress among healthcare workers (Darboe et al., 2016). They concluded that high perceived effort-reward imbalance among HCWs, better incentives, and reasonable allocation of resources for healthcare workers would help prevent stress at work.

Potter, Gonzalez, and Xu (2015) conducted a quantitative study in Sierra Leone, West Africa to determine heat stress among HCWs treating patients with the Ebola virus disease. Potter et al. indicated that HCWs in Sierra Leone, West Africa were required to wear personal protective clothing (PPC); however, because of the heat, HCWs still complained of heat stress. According to the study, heat stress can affect HCWs' performance at work and can also be deadly. The study was conducted in West Africa during the EVD outbreak with the aim of producing a stress-free environment for healthcare workers combating the Ebola virus disease. The researchers used a sweating thermal manikin to measure operating resistance among healthcare workers. The researchers indicated that there was a rise in body temperature among healthcare workers. They found that heat exhaustion occurs between 37°C and 40°C and heatstroke prevents HCWs from providing quality care for their clients. They concluded that HCWs caring for patients with the EVD need personal cooling systems to create a safe and stress-free work environment.

The studies addressed in the section above clearly indicate that stress among HCWs cannot be ignored. Raab et al. (2015) concluded that stress affects how HCWs perform their jobs. Shoji et al. (2014) suggested the need for effective mental health programs to help HCWs with self-efficacy and perceived social support. Ding et al. (2014) concluded that burnout causes both occupational stress and anxiety symptoms. Selamu et al. (2017) recommended a better understanding of job-related stress and burnout among healthcare workers. Darboe et al. (2016) recommended better incentives for HCWs while Potter et al. (2015) called for better cooling systems for healthcare workers.

However, these existing literatures do not provide information on HCWs mental health while providing care for patients with the Ebola virus disease. Most of the studies found that stress can affect the performance of HCWs, and Ding et al. (2014) further addressed some of the specific symptoms, such as anxiety and depression, exhibited by healthcare workers when they are under stress. Most of the studies cited the importance of dealing with stress so that HCWs can provide quality care for their clients. Some of the studies recommended that additional effective measures are needed to help HCWs with stress at work. Finally, these studies confirmed that the impact of stress among HCWs should not be ignored and effective stress management measures are needed to help HCWs provide adequate care for their patients. However, there has been no study on how HCWs cope with stress while providing treatments to the Ebola virus patients in Freetown, Sierra Leoneans. Therefore, how do HCWs of Freetown, Sierra Leone cope with stress during the EVD while working with highly infectious patients is relevant to this study? This was an area that was explored in this study. Reviewing additional literature that provides information on HCWs and coping was significant for this study. As a result, I addressed Literature to HCWs and coping in the next paragraph.

Healthcare Workers and Coping

The lack of effective coping skills can affect the performance of HCWs, especially when working with highly contagious patients. Jordan, Khubchandani, and Wiblishauser (2016) examined the impact of perceived stress and coping adequacy among healthcare workers.

They conducted a cross-sectional study in the Midwestern United States and gathered data from 174 participants using a quantitative survey method. The study found that HCWs used effective and positive methods to cope with stress. Some of the methods were talking to friends, meditating, listening to music, and watching television. They reported that there was no statistical significance across selected demographic variables on self-reported coping ability. However, the study found that 42% of healthcare workers cope poorly with stress. The study concluded that both stress and the lack of coping abilities affect the quality of services provided by healthcare workers.

Fernandes and Nirmala (2017) conducted a qualitative study in India on workplace stress and coping strategies among healthcare workers. They indicated that increased levels of stress and burnout among HCWs contributed to high turnover among healthcare workers. The study indicated that there would be shortages of HCWs by the year 2020 if better coping strategies are not implemented for healthcare workers. They investigated work stress and coping strategies among 51 HCWs working at the Goa hospital in India. Occupational stress is an emotional state of mind (Lee & Wang, 2002).

Lee and Wang indicated that occupational stress causes HCWs to feel as if they are not meeting their employers' demands. They also found that major stress resulted in high turnover among healthcare workers. That is, some HCWs were leaving their jobs because of high stress. They found that the coping strategies used include avoidance of the problem, mental disengagement, problem- solving/planning, speech coping and social support.

Saini, Kaur, and Das (2016) conducted a study among 285 HCWs in both a general unit and an intensive care unit (ICU) in India. The data were collected using the modified work stress symptom scale (WSS) and coping checklist (CCL). They found that HCWs experienced different kinds of stresses. HCWs working in the ICU experienced a moderate level of stress. They found that the primary coping strategies used by HCWs were problem-solving and religion. The study noted that there had been only four other studies conducted on coping skills in India, which suggests that it may not be relevant to HCWs in other parts of the world.

Koh et al. (2015) conducted a cross-sectional study in Singapore to determine the use of coping mechanisms among HCWs in connection with burnout and psychological morbidity. The participants in this study were doctors, nurses, and social workers. A total of 493 participants were included in the study. Cases of prevailing burnout were reported by 3.3%; 91 of the 292 participants complained of burnout. The study found that HCWs who had coping mechanisms complained less of psychological morbidity and burnout. The study also found that HCWs used the following coping mechanisms to prevent workplace burnout: physical well-being, clinical variety, hobbies, and meditation. HCWs in Singapore used spirituality and family relationships as coping strategies. Koh et al. concluded that there is a high prevalence of burnout among HCWSs in Singapore as compared to HCWs in other parts of the world. However, HCWs in Singapore with effective coping strategies adjusted well to workplace burnout.

Howlett et al. (2015) conducted a quantitative, cross-sectional study in Canada on how HCWs in the emergency department cope with burnout. They used Linear regression with the Coping Inventory for Stressful Situation (CISS) and the Maslach Burnout Inventory (MBI) to evaluate the coping styles of 616 emergency staff. The study used CISS to measure coping styles in three categories: task-oriented, emotion-oriented, and avoidance-oriented coping. The study found that task-oriented coping is related to decreases risk of burnout, whereas, emotion-oriented coping is related to increased risk of burnout. They concluded that coping style intervention might reduce burnout, which would foster staff well-being. Howlett et al. (2015) commented that future studies should "focus on building and sustaining task-oriented coping, along with an alternative to emotion-oriented coping" (p. 5).

Petrites, Mullan, Spangenberg, and Gold (2016) examined how healthcare workers in Ghana, West Africa cope with high rates of perinatal death. They indicated that perinatal mortality affects the well-being of healthcare workers as well as the patient care they provide. The authors conducted semi-structured interviews among healthcare workers at a hospital in Kumasi, Ghana and included 36 participants—comprised of midwives, pediatricians, and physicians—in the study. The researchers used content analysis to identify nine themes that emerged from the study. Participants reported that they learned to cope by understanding the meaning of their clients' deaths. Participants also recognized their ability to be an agent of change and demonstrated emotional engagement in response to perinatal death.

Participants noted that they developed multiple coping skills related to their clients' deaths. The study found that 42% of HCWs noted that a lack of resources contributed to their clients' deaths. They also claimed that the lack of medical equipment contributed to their lack of coping skills. Of the HCWs studied, 22% reported believing that God was responsible for the deaths of their clients and 52% indicated that they try not to think about the deaths of their clients. However, 72% of HCWs reported symptoms of emotional impact and 72% of HCWs developed coping mechanisms to deal with the loss of their clients. The study concluded that HCWs in low-resource countries, especially Saharan Africa, demonstrated high resiliency in coping with perinatal death. Petrites et al. (2016) recommended that additional research should be conducted concerning coping strategies for HCWs to strengthen their self- efficacy and engagement. These studies together confirmed that effective coping skills are needed for healthcare workers even when they are not working with highly contagious patients.

Additionally, Qiao et al. (2016) conducted a study on occupational burnout and coping among HCWs who care for patients with HIV/AIDS in China. The cross-sectional study included 264 HCWs caring for patients with HIV/AIDS and an additional 228 physicians and nurses caring for patients with other infectious diseases. The researchers conducted a quantitative study using a self-administered questionnaire, Maslach Burnout Inventory-General Survey (MBI -GS), the Symptom Checklist 90 (SCL-90), the Eysenck Personality Questionnaire (EPQ), and Trait Coping Style Questionnaire (TCSQ). They found that HCWs with HIV/AIDS scored higher on markers of emotional exhaustion and depersonalization than other healthcare workers. They also found that HCWs with HIV/AIDS used negative coping skills, which affected their work performance. They concluded that 76.9% of HCWs met the criteria for burnout.

Because of their role, HCWs experience tremendous stress, which can lead to long-term psychological difficulties (Khalid et al., 2016). Khalid et al. postulated that it was evident that HCWs were under extreme stress during the MERS-COV outbreaks. They found that, during the MERS-COV epidemic, HCWs experienced emotional difficulties including anxiety and nervousness. They indicated that some of the stressors HCWs experienced during the MERS-COV outbreak were related to safety concerns. HCWs observed patients and coworkers die in their presence and were therefore concerned about transmitting the disease to their friends and family. They also found that two of the factors that helped HCWs cope with the MERS-COV outbreak were positive attitudes and following strict precautions of safety standards.

Bangura, Lynch, and Binns (2013) evaluated the impact of coping strategies in the rural area of Kono in the Kambia district of Sierra Leone. The study found that all 250 of the participants were resilient to climatic conditions, despite the lack of adequate support from the government. The study concluded that external support is needed in Sierra Leone, especially during an epidemic or crisis. This study did not report findings related to healthcare workers' coping strategies. However, it provided relevant information on coping strategies of Sierra Leoneans in West Africa.

These studies together confirmed that effective coping methods are needed when working with highly contagious patients. Further, the studies reviewed indicated that factors such as inadequate resources in poor nations affect effective coping strategies for healthcare workers. These studies have encouraged policymakers to incorporate strategies that will help HCWs to develop effective coping skills. Therefore, how HCWs cope with stress while working with infectious patients in a poor-quality healthcare system applies to this study. Asking participants about their stress and coping in addition to the mental health issues and treatment they experienced was relevant to this study. This is an area I intend to explore.

Because stress is bad and leads to mental health issues and numerous coping strategies are helpful, reviewing additional literature that provides information on barriers to mental health was significant for this study. Thus, literature addressing barriers to mental healthcare is discussed in the next paragraph.

Barriers to Mental Health Care

Good mental health enables individuals to be productive in society and poor mental health is a significant problem in today's society. One of the barriers to good mental health for HCWs in the West African nation is the lack of optimal mental health care (Gwaikolo et al., 2017). Another barrier associated with mental illness in Africa is stigmatization (Taghva et al., 2017).

Oexle et al. (2015) examined perceived need as a barrier to mental health among members in the community healthcare in Africa. They cited that the refusal of mental healthcare is a burden for individuals with mental illness. They conducted a quantitative study using the Brief Illness Perception Questionnaire to assess participants' symptoms related to mental illness and the Self Appraisal of Illness Questionnaire to measure participants' perceived need for mental health care. They surveyed 202 participants between the ages of 20 -41 with distress symptoms. They found that perceived need for mental health care was moderate. However, participants reported perceived barriers, such as stigma, as being low. Oexle et al. (2015) found that perceived need for mental illness treatment was related to increased stigma. They also found that increased stigma was a barrier for most of the participants. They concluded that an intervention of increased mental health services would help change the attitude of individuals experiencing mental health crises. They argued that stigmatization is one of the main barriers to mental illness. Even though the study did not include healthcare workers as participants, the findings are relevant to our purposes regarding the barriers associated with mental health care in Africa.

Weiss and Amie (2017) conducted a quantitative research study using an online survey to examine barriers to global health development. They invited 432 healthcare workers to participate in the study, with a participation rate of 62% (268 participants). They conducted descriptive and inferential statistics and found that 34/66 barriers were global challenges for mental health care. They found perceived social and culture as barriers to mental health services. The study concluded that mental health barriers have a tremendous effect on both individual and system levels. The researchers hoped that the 22 barriers found in this study could create a solution that will address the global mental health crisis.

Rugema, Krantz, Mogren, Ntaganira, and Persson (2015) conducted a qualitative study addressing mental health barriers at a mental health hospital in southern Rwanda, South Africa and at a psychosocial center within the capital city of Kigali. They used a qualitative approach with six focus group discussions (FGD) to evaluate 43 HCWs, both men and women. They found that there was a constant struggle among Rwandans who received mental health care and cited some of the related barriers: "Poverty and lack of family support, fear of stigmatization, poor community awareness of mental disorder, societal believe in traditional healers and prayers, scarce resources in mental health care, and Gender imbalance" (Rugema et al., 2015, p. 5). However, individuals in Rwanda who are privileged enough to have good insurance were able to get successful mental health treatment.

Umubyeyi, Mogren, Ntaganira, and Krantz (2016) conducted a study to investigate the barriers to care and self-efficacy among young adults with depression and suicidality in low-income areas of Rwanda, South Africa. The cross-sectional study used two samples: 247 participants suffering from depression and 502 participants suffering from other mental illness. They measured self-seeking behavior as a barrier to care and self-efficacy for mental health care. They used logistic regression to identify risk factors associated with barriers. They found that 30% of participants with depression and suicidality asked for mental health care and 64% asked for help from people they trusted.

However, the study found that only six people reached out for mental health care from experienced professionals. The key barriers identified were limited accessibility and acceptability of mental healthcare services. The population experiencing depression and suicidality also expressed low confidence to seek mental health care. However, individuals had high levels of confidence to talk about their mental health problems. Umubyeyi et al. (2016) concluded that the study's population experienced limited access to mental health care and encouraged mental health literacy for the population.

Gwaikolo et al. (2017) conducted another study in Liberia, West Africa. They employed a mixed methods approach, which involves both quantitative and qualitative methods. They collected data from 22 HCWs at 19 rural healthcare facilities over the course of six focus groups and semi-structured assessment of 19 primary healthcare facilities. They found several potential barriers affecting mental health treatment in Liberia, West Africa, which included:

> Lack of mental health knowledge among plan by healthcare staff, the high workload for plan healthcare workers, additional mental health responsibilities, lack of mental health drugs, the poor physical infrastructure of health facilities...poor communication

> support including the lack of electricity and mobile phone, negative attitude and stigma towards people with severe mental disorders…and stigma against mental healthcare workers. (p. 5)

They concluded that Liberia should improve the barriers to mental health care in West Africa and must improve their infrastructure and the attitude of the population toward mental illness.

Hann, Pearson, Campbell, Sesay, and Eaton (2015) examined barriers to mental health in Freetown, Makeni, Sierra Leone, West Africa. They conducted a quantitative study among low-income individuals. The study used grounded theory to guide the study of 24 participants. They found that the barriers to mental health care were the lack of mental health networking and lack of political will. They suggested creating a policy to advocate for quality mental health care in Sierra Leone and help provide quality mental health care. The study also identified a need to increase awareness of mental health. Hann, Pearson, Campbell, Sesay, and Eaton concluded the study by indicating that networking and the lack of political help from the government are the major barriers to mental healthcare in Sierra Leone, West Africa.

The above studies clearly identify that there are several barriers to mental health care. Rugema et al. (2015) provided information about the struggle of Africans to accept mental health diagnoses because of stigmatization. They found that poverty and stigma are barriers to mental health care in Africa. Umubyeyi et al. (2016) indicated that there are limited accessibility and acceptability of mental health care in Africa. Gwaikolo et al. (2017) found that the lack of psychotropic medication and poor infrastructure are barriers to mental healthcare in Africa. Hann et al. (2015) found the lack of political will in Sierra Leone as a barrier to mental health. These studies indicated that stigmatization, poverty, acceptability, accessibility, the lack of psychotropic medication, and the lack of political influence are the significant barriers to the mental healthcare system.

On the contrary, Oexle et al. (2015) used specific measures to address the barriers to mental health care. They found that one of the barriers to mental health care is stigmatization. The study provided general information related to mental illness. Weiss and Amie (2017) provided specific information on barriers to global health development and addressed 22 barriers related to mental health. These studies addressed specific barriers to mental health care, findings which will encourage policymakers to address the barriers related to mental health care. However, the existing literature did not address HCWs' perspectives on mental health symptoms they experienced while caring for patients with the Ebola virus. The study also found that inadequate resources for HCWs, especially during an epidemic like the Ebola virus disease as a barrier to mental healthcare. Therefore, the next paragraph addressed epidemic and healthcare workers.

Epidemic and Healthcare Workers

The EVD outbreak of 2014 to 2015 was an epidemic that resulted in the deaths of many healthcare workers. The CDC (2014) cited that the epidemics of the EVD involved human contact between body fluid of infected animals. According to the CDC, when an individual is infected or dies, the virus continues to spread to other individuals who encounter the infected individual's body fluid or blood. The CDC postulated that HCWs accidentally die when working with the EVD patients.

HCWs are at an increased risk to be infected with the influenza virus. The CDC (2014) and the WHO (2016) cited that the epidemic of the influenza virus occurs yearly, and it is a respiratory illness that is caused by Influenza A or B virus. According to the CDC (2014), the influenza virus is seasonal, that is, the virus spreads during the winter seasons. The spread of the influenza virus depends on the population that is susceptible to the virus. The CDC (2016) postulated that HCWs are a high-risk population for the influenza virus.

HCWs are at an increased risk to be infected with the human immunodeficiency virus (HIV). Engel et al. (2017) did a qualitative study on a diagnostic practice on HIV patients in South Africa. They found that information provided by healthcare workers is relevant to implement better strategies to combat infectious diseases. They stated that HCWs indicated that the strategies used to combat HIV were ineffective. The knowledge of HCWs is relevant to make clinical decisions (Eckes, 2016). A qualitative study is one-way knowledge can be interpreted and translated to make a clinical decision because it involves individuals lived experiences (Biswas et al., 2008). Joyce,

Kuhar, and Brooks (2015) cited that the epidemic of the HIV is transmitted through occupational exposure to blood, body fluids, and viral cultures. According to the WHO (2015), HCWs should use preventive measures because they work with a vulnerable population that can spread the immunodeficiency virus.

Ansumana et al. (2017) postulated that 28% of the 9.6 million new cases of tuberculosis are found in the African region. They stated that the spread of the EVD of 2014 and 2015 affected the tuberculosis healthcare system and HCWs in Sierra Leone, Liberia, and Guinea. They found that the spread of the EVD Killed doctors, nurses, ambulance drivers, porters, and community organizers. The WHO (2016) reported that the spread of the EVD killed 328 HCWs in Sierra Leone, 288 HCWs in Liberia, and 199 HCWs in Guinea. Ansumana et al. postulated that the spread of the EVD weakened the healthcare system in West Africa.

These studies together confirmed that HCWs are the most vulnerable population to an epidemic because they work with highly contagious patients. Further, the literature reviewed recommended protective measures and vaccinations for HCWs during an epidemic. These studies have encouraged policymakers to incorporate strategies that would help HCWs to receive yearly vaccinations and employ effective measures during an epidemic. An epidemic is bad and could lead to stress, and the deaths of healthcare workers and proper preventive measures are needed. Therefore, how do HCWs cope with the EVD while providing treatments to the Ebola virus patients in Freetown, Sierra Leoneans was the area that was explored in this study.

Summary and Conclusion

Creswell (2009) and Patton (2002) recommended the need for selecting the right literature and theoretical work for a study. The literature review for this study showed that HCWs in Africa during the EVD experienced mixed mental health symptoms that need to be investigated. Some of the quantitative studies in the literature provide vital information related to the mental health of healthcare workers during an epidemic. After a comprehensive review of the literature, it was evident that the mental health of HCWs needs to be studied to help provide adequate mental health care for them during an outbreak or an epidemic. Based on the existing data, the literature review utilized quantitative research (Li et al., 2015; Scott et al., 2009); whereas, qualitative research has not been used to study the mental health of HCWs during the EVD outbreak of 2014 to 2015. Creswell (2009) cited that qualitative study provides an in-depth understanding of a phenomenon. Fasina et al. (2015) utilized the qualitative research method during the EVD to examine the health care system in West Africa.

A similar study conducted by Brolin Ribacke et al. (2016) used a qualitative methodology to examine the health care system in Sierra Leone, West Africa. Another qualitative study by Khalid et al. (2016) examined how HCWs cope with the cases of the MERS –COV outbreak in Saudi Arabia. Hughes (2015) also utilized a qualitative study to explore the mental health system in Sierra Leone, West Africa. These studies utilized a qualitative method to get an in-depth understanding of how HCWs cope with the mental health system.

I reviewed and divided the literature into different topics. The findings of this literature were helpful to understand the health care system and HCWs in Africa. However, the studies failed to provide information about how HCWs in Freetown, Sierra Leone describe their mental health symptoms they experienced and how they used coping skills when treating patients with the Ebola virus. The next chapter of the study elaborates on the methodology that was used. Because HCWs are the first responders to an epidemic, it was essential to understand the experiences and perceptions of their mental health during an epidemic. Chapter 3 expands on the qualitative design of the study to describe HCWs perspectives on their mental health when treating EVD patients. Chapter 3 includes the introduction, the research design, and rationale for the design, the role of the researcher, methodology, participants' selection, instrumentation for recruitment, participation, data collection, and analysis plan. Issues of trustworthiness and ethical procedures were also discussed. Chapter 3 ends with a summary and a highlight of Chapter 4.

CHAPTER 3

Research Method

Introduction

The purpose of this study was to explore HCWs' perspectives on their mental health symptoms during the 2014 and 2015 EVD outbreak in Freetown, Sierra Leone. Chapter 1 provided an overview of this research, and Chapter 2 addressed the theoretical framework that was used in this study. In addition, Chapter 2 focused on a literature review that identified the gap in the study. Chapter 3 of the study addresses the research design, the role played by the researcher, the methodology used in this study, issues of trustworthiness, and ethical implications related to this study.

Research Design and Rationale

Research Questions

>   RQ1. How do HCWs in Freetown, Sierra Leone describe their lived experiences regarding their own mental health when treating patients with Ebola virus disease?

RQ2. How do HCWs feel with their abilities to cope with stress while treating patients with the Ebola virus disease?

RQ3. How do HCWs describe their lived experiences of the mental health care treatment they received while treating patients with the Ebola virus disease?

Phenomenon

Creswell (2009) asserted that research designs enable researchers to select the right method for a study. The phenomenon that was explored in this study was HCWs' perspectives on their mental health symptoms during the EVD outbreak of 2014 and 2015. Creswell (2009) asserted that it is imperative that a researcher select a research design that addresses the goal of his or her study. Phenomenological research design was selected for this study. Phenomenological research design fosters an inductive approach, which allows the researcher to begin with the data and explore what is going on in a particular place (Patton, 2002). This design enabled me to address the phenomenon being studied and answer the research questions.

Role of the Researcher

According to Creswell (2009) and Patton (2002), qualitative researchers are required to select the right instrument that is valid and reliable when collecting data. Denzin and Lincoln (2003) and Greenbank (2003) postulated that interview questions are the instruments in qualitative research data collection. The interview questions served as the primary instrument in conducting face-to-face interviews with the participants in a natural setting, and I served as the researcher. Researchers play several roles in qualitative research (Creswell, 2009; Patton, 2002). These roles are observing participants, acting as a participant observer, and conducting in-depth interviews or remaining neutral. My role as a researcher was to recruit and select the right participants for this study. Additionally, my role included interviewing participants, gathering data, and completing and interpreting the data analysis. I did not have any personal or professional relationships with the participants. In this study, I used in-depth interviewing to gather information on the phenomenon of interest. Time was properly used to make sure the data were collected and reviewed effectively.

Because I am from Freetown, Sierra Leone, it was imperative that I avoid all biases associated with the study. I was aware that cultural perspectives play a significant role in the diagnosis of mental illness in Africa. I was also aware that any form of bias or prejudice would easily compromise my study. Therefore, I was openminded concerning any issues related to prejudice or bias during the study. Additionally, I sought to measure any biases or power relationships that I had as the researcher by employing bracketing. Husserl (1967) postulated that bracketing is the act of suspending all judgement and focusing on participants lived experience. I used bracketing as a phenomenological analysis in the following ways: I approached the study without bias or judgment (Husserl, 1967). I suspended the truth in the objective world (Jarvis, 2013). I was able to set aside any assumptions, revisit the data, and gain a full understanding of the study. Bracketing was crucial for me because I was born in Freetown, Sierra Leone, and my background experience could have affected my judgment.

Methodology

Participant Selection

The present study was focused on the perceptions of HCWs who provided care to patients during the 2014 and 2015 EVD outbreak. The sample was drawn from HCWs in the western area in Freetown, Sierra Leone who cared for Ebola victims. HCWs were given invitational letters (see Appendix A) asking them to participate in the study.

Sampling

Purposeful sampling was used to select participants for this study. According to Patton (2002) and Verial (2013), purposeful sampling gives researchers the opportunity to select a specific group or a particular population for a study. This method is used to gather in-depth information from a particular group. As such, HCWs in Freetown, Sierra Leone who worked with EVD patients were selected for this study. The participants were directly selected from the western area of Freetown, Sierra Leone. The selected area includes the main hospital called Connaught, which is located at 6 Lamina Sankoh Street in Freetown. Participants were recruited by invitational letters (see Appendix A). Most of the HCWs had been employed at this hospital during the EVD outbreak. The capital city was chosen because of the different social and economic background in terms of its diversity of the people. In addition, Freetown, Sierra Leone has more qualified HCWs than the provinces of the country. Individuals leave the provinces to seek a better life in the capital city of Freetown. The selected participants were all Africans who shared the same cultural values.

As such, individuals who were selected for the study had direct experience in working with highly infectious patients. These individuals were able to voice their opinions about their mental health symptoms while providing care for patients with EVD. Participation in this study occurred on a voluntary basis.

Sample Size

The sample size was determined by the type of study being conducted. According to Creswell (2009), a sample of five to 20 participants can be studied using a phenomenological design. Morse (1994) indicated that a sample of six participants is appropriate for a phenomenological design. Because of the above recommendation, 10 participants were selected for this study. I used an additional 10 participants in case participants dropped out of the study. I also focused on saturation during the interview process. Saturation occurs when adequate data have been collected for analysis (Creswell, 2009).

The following criteria were used to select participants for this study.

- Participants were both male and female adult HCWs who had treated EVD patients during the 2014 and 2015 EVD outbreak in Freetown, Sierra Leone.

- All participants had resided in Freetown, Sierra Leone for at least 5years.
- All participants spoke English (English is one of the languages spoken in the area where participants were recruited).
- All participants were willing to participate in a study on issues related to their mental health symptoms during the EVD outbreak of 2014 and 2015.

Instrumentation

Interviews are based on the development of relationships between participants and the researcher (Brew &Kottler, 2008). To interview participants, I used semi structured interview questions. I conducted interviews in a calm and a non-distracting environment (Ivey, 2000). I strived to be genuine and to serve as an empathetic listener during the interview process. Patton (2002) contended that building rapport is important in ensuring an effective interview. To build rapport with the participants, I was not emotional, and I sought to provide a calm atmosphere during the interviews. This study was conducted at a café outside of Connaught Hospital at6 Lamina Sankoh Street in the western area of Freetown, Sierra Leone. I conducted interviews at a location near where participants had experienced the problems of interest to the study. This location was chosen because it was less restrictive and separate from participants' actual place of employment. To capture participants' experiences and to get in-depth information on their mental health during the EVD outbreak, Connaught Hospital was used as the main site.

I explained the purpose of the interview to all participants. I explained the rules of confidentiality and the length of the interview to all the participants. Participants were encouraged to leave their contact information after this study in case further information was needed.

I recorded one interview per respondent for at least 45 minutes. I used interview questions in this study. Additionally, I used the following guidelines recommended by Creswell (2009) fora phenomenological interview:

- Researchers are to understand the philosophical understanding of the participants;

- Researchers are to collect data only from participants who have experienced the phenomenon;
- Researchers are to employ a phenomenological approach to analyze the data during the interviews, and
- Researchers are to employ a reduction method in data analysis.

I conducted in-depth interviews with open-ended questions. I described the concept or phenomenon of individual lived experiences directly to the participants (Moustakas, 1994). I applied the recommendations of Moustakas (1994) for in-depth interviews in phenomenological inquiries by doing the following:

- I focused on the lived experience of the individual or the phenomenon of interest,
- I focused on present experiences, and
- I combined the first and second experiences of HCWs to understand the phenomenon of interest.

Field Notes

To gather data in an efficient manner, I used field notes (Patton, 2002), which then provided additional layers of data that I could properly analyze (Creswell, 2009). I avoided gathering data that were not relevant to the study (Patton, 2002). To document participants' responses to the interview questions at the research site, field notes were incorporated as a tool. Using the field notes, I was able to categorize common themes related to the research problem underpinning the study. Creswell (2009) recommended that field notes consist of both reflective and descriptive information. Therefore, I documented factual data during the interviews in addition to recording my thoughts, ideas, and concerns.

Researcher-Developed Instruments

I developed open-ended, semi structured, in-depth questions to gather a full understanding of HCWs' perceptions of their mental health while providing treatment for EVD patients. The questions were developed based on the literature review regarding HCWs' perceptions when working with highly infectious patients. Appendix B provides the interview questions for this study. All interviews were tape recorded and transcribed for data analysis.

Content validity was established by communicating with the participants to capture and understand their perspectives related to the research questions and the research topic (Creswell, 2009). According to Patton (1990), a qualitative content analysis provides patterns, themes, and categories for a study, where coding becomes the fundamental analytic process in a qualitative content analysis. However, van Manen (2017) recognized that phenomenology is not about instrumentalities and technicalities but involves a search for deep understanding of the lived experiences of individuals. van Manen contended that phenomenology is the practice of both scholar-practitioners and quotidian practitioners. For instance, a thoughtful understanding of the everyday lives of people is of great value to scholar-practitioners. He also pointed out that phenomenology is an approach that differs from other types of inquiry.

Procedures for Recruitment, Participation, and Data Collection

Procedures for recruitment and data collection started after I received Institutional Review Board (IRB) approval from Walden and signed consent forms from the selected participants. A purposeful sample of 10 participants was selected through the use of invitation letters (see Appendix A). I obtained contact information from all individuals who wanted to take part in the study.

I collected data through interviews and field notes. All data were collected at 6 Lamina Sankoh Street in Freetown, Sierra Leone. According to Turner (2010) and Creswell (2009), there are different types of interview techniques. I collected data using semi structured interview questions (see Appendix B). I used this approach to ask open- ended questions. Participants were given the opportunity to unfold their views and understanding of the phenomenon during the interviews (Creswell, 2009). Data collection and analysis were conducted at the same time (Merriam, 1998). Data collection occurred at a location close to where participants had experienced the problem of interest. All of the data were collected and organized into categories of themes.

Semi structured interviews enable researchers to interact with participants (Creswell, 2009). The incorporation of semi structured interviews in research, according to Creswell (2009), enables researchers to be attentive and to provide in-depth information on the phenomenon being studied. This method enabled me to pause, give participants the opportunity to express themselves freely, and control the questions being asked. Semi structured interviews in this study enabled me to follow a set of instructions that produced reliable, comparable qualitative data. However, face-to-face semi structured data collection has some limitations. Specifically, indirect information can be filtered by the interviewees' perspectives, and the information is provided ina designated setting (Creswell, 2009). To explore any issue that might have been difficult for participants to explain, I asked additional questions (Creswell, 2009). Creswell contended that not all participants are able to properly elaborate on their perceptions of their own lived experiences.

Interview Guide Protocol

An interview guide enabled me to use the same basic line of inquiry with each participant who was interviewed (Patton, 2002). I used the interview guide (see Appendix B)to explore, probe, and ask questions that enabled participants to explore their lived experiences (Patton, 2002). As an interviewer, I sought to manage my time efficiently when using the interview guide questions (Patton, 2002). I kept my interactions with the interviewees focused until their perspectives and experiences emerged.

Patton (2002) postulated that interviews begin with the notion that individuals have valuable lived experiences that they might want to share. Creswell (2009) and Moustakas (1994) stated that phenomenological study is the process of collecting data through interviewing. Individuals may process and experience things differently. The interview questions were generated from the following research questions:

RQ1. How do HCWs in Freetown, Sierra Leone describe their lived experiences regarding their own mental health when treating patients with Ebola virus disease?

RQ2. How do HCWs feel with their abilities to cope with stress while treating patients with the Ebola virus disease?

RQ3. How do HCWs describe their lived experiences of the mental health care treatment they received while treating patients with the Ebola virus disease?

The first semi structured interview question that addressed RQ1 was "Describe for me your mental health when treating patients with the Ebola virus disease." I asked this question to engage participants by prompting them to provide a full narrative of their mental health (Creswell, 2009; Patton, 2002) when treating patients with EVD. The second interview question, whichaddressedRQ2, was "Talk to me about how you responded or coped with the death of your patients, friends, or family members." The third interview question, whichaddressedRQ3, was "What specific support do you think will be helpful in relieving stress when working with highly infectious patients, such as Ebola virus disease patients?" I also used a follow-up interview question to address RQ3:"How will effective mental healthcare improve your work performance, especially during an epidemic like the EVD outbreak?" These questions enabled participants to reflect on the need for adequate mental health care during an epidemic and to start a dialogue for quality mental health care in Freetown, Sierra Leone. The last question was "What does it feel like to be a participant in this study?" This question was presented in recognition of the importance of a debriefing period. Further, this question gave participants the opportunity to share any experiences they might have forgotten to include, as well as to ask questions related to the study.

In a phenomenological study, researchers sometimes need more information than they get from the participants. Therefore, it's essential that researchers employ strategies when interviewing participants (Patton, 2002). Rubin and Rubin (1995) contended that the modification of questions and researchers' calmness and flexibility would enable researchers to be receptive to what the participant is saying. Probing allowed participants to provide in-depth information about their feelings, personal opinions, and there use of critical thinking (Rubin &Rubin, 1995). Probing in interview provides the following three purposes. These purposes are (a) it improves the depth of the interview, (b) it enables the interviewee to provide more details, and (c) it gives reassurance to the interviewer that the interviewee is listening (Rubin & Rubin, 1995). Therefore, probing was necessary on this study, as it gave participants the opportunity to provide in-depth information during the interviews, I also used probes to prompt participants to provide full narratives of their lived experiences when providing care for Ebola virus patients.

I interviewed each participant on different days. All data was recorded by audio tape. I checked the audio tape to ensure that the interview process was being recorded efficiently and effectively. In qualitative data recording procedure, I examined the recording information to make sure that I was recording the correct information for the study (Creswell, 2009; Patton, 2002). The advantage of audio recording data collection enables researchers to collect data from participants without being obstructed (Creswell, 2009). The recruitment resulted in 10 participants; therefore, I did not develop a compensation strategy that adequately reimburses participants to participate in the study.

Also, I networked with healthcare staff who were not affiliated with the research to help cultivate sources of referral to recruit participants.

Debriefing Procedures

Before participants exit the study, they were assured that all information disclosed in the study would remain confidential. But also, participants were informed that results from the data collected in this study would be shared with mental health providers to help them understand the need for quality mental health care during an epidemic, such as the EVD outbreak. In addition, participants were encouraged to provide contact information in case I have follow-up questions. Participants were also informed that the result of this study would be provided to them through their emails.

Data Analysis Plan

Polit and Beck (2006) stated that the main aspect of data analysis is to provide a detailed description of the experiences and perceptions of individuals. For this study, I analyzed how HCWs in Freetown, Sierra Leone described their lived experiences regarding their own mental health when treating patients with EVD? Specific interview questions for each RQ are shown in Appendix B. I was able to ask specific open-ended questions that narrowed the scope of the study. I also used inductive data analysis to build patterns, categories, and themes from the bottom up (Patton, 2002). In an inductive approach, as I read through all the data, encoding the data, themes emerged from this study. I worked back and forth between the themes and the database until I established a comprehensive set of themes.

Open coding was used to look for distinct concepts and the data to develop first level categories, as well as second (third, fourth, etc.) level codes that are associated and coded to the primary codes. At the first level of coding, I looked for distinct concepts in the data to form the basic categories or units of analysis. Three rounds of coding were done.

I uploaded my transcribed interviews into NVivo 10 to create themes from the participants. I used NVivo 10 to code all transcripts and to open all the themes by double clicking on the themes. To display participants coded quotes, I used NVivo 10 and the most common themes were transcribed from NVivo into words. I then copied each of the quotes that applied to the individual theme from NVivo and transcribed it into Word. According to Hsiung (2008), reflexivity challenges researchers to explain how their emotions, personal beliefs, assumptions, and subject location affect the research process. To present my findings in Chapter 4, I included the applicable participant quotes from each theme. The manner of treatment of discrepant cases was addressed by using a color- coded system to highlight specific themes before data analysis. Erickson (2012) postulated that color coding is an effective manner to treat discrepancies during research. Erickson also posited that triangulation is an effective strategy for data collection. This researcher used triangulation as a manner of treatment of discrepant cases.

Issues of Trustworthiness

According to Shenton (2004), trustworthiness in a study includes credibility, transferability, dependability, and confirmability. In this study, credibility was achieved by ensuring validity. That was, I measured what I set out to measure. I understood participant's views on their mental health symptoms they experienced during the EVD outbreak. To maintain internal validity, I used the following strategies: (a) member checking–I asked participants to review my interpretation to foster truth and validity of the data (Creswell, 2009). Through member checks, I gave participants the opportunity to remove any information not suitable for future publication. Participants were required to sign a consent form for the release of information. I verified the clarification of researchers' bias, which was found in the proposal under researcher's role that described the relevant aspect of the research (Denzin & Lincoln, 2008). Finally, (c) I collected data through interviews and field notes (Creswell, 2009).

Denzin and Lincoln (2003) postulated that transferability is demonstrated when the study applies to other populations. I provided full description of the population that the reader would use as a guide to understand that the finding could be used to other population or situation (Denzin& Lincoln, 1994). Also, I made sure that other researchers researching HCWs mental health during the EVD outbreak are able to understand the findings of this study.

Dependability would enable other researchers to use my research study for research purposes, as noted in my data analysis plan. I demonstrated that if the study was repeated over time, employing similar methods, context as well as participants, the similar results would be obtained (Denzin & Lincoln, 2003). Also, I worked with my chair and committee member to ensure that the result of this study is from HCWs perspectives and not from my own opinion.

Confirmability involves researchers' concerns for objectivity (Shenton, 2004). I maintained a nonbiased position and allowed participants to retell their lived experiences. Further, I established reliability by employing three techniques. First, I provided information on the focus of the study; my role and position as a researcher, and how the data are be gathered (Creswell, 2009; Patton, 1990). Second, I ensured that the data analysis and the data collection provide a clear picture of the study being conducted. I also expect the study to be scrutinized by experienced qualitative researchers. Also, reliability involves the repetition of the phenomenon being studied (Morse, 1994; Patton, 2002). Therefore, I conducted a final audit at the end of my study to make sure that the study was efficiently and effectively done.

Ethical Procedures

Walden University Institutional Review Board (2008) indicated that researchers are to maintain the highest standards when conducting research involving human subjects. Walden University Review Board indicated that researchers are always to be ethical during the research. Also, Walden University IRB strongly discourages the collection of any data before the approval from the International Review Board. This would enable Walden University IRB to approve all current and future use of ethical issues before collecting data. Application for IRB approval was obtained before data collection. The application for permission from the IRB was included after I received approval from the IRB on September 11, 2018. Walden University Institutional Review Board approval number is 09-11-18-0319268, which is included in the informed consent form.

To address the treatment of human participation, I employed the National Institutes of Health (NIH; see Appendix C) privacy rule to let participants know that this rule upholds the rules of confidentiality. Ethical concerns related to recruitment materials and processes and a plan were addressed by upholding IRB recommendation and APA ethical standards. The IRB recommended that all data collected are to be stored in a safe place to promote confidentiality. Creswell (2009) indicated that researchers inform participants that their participation is strictly voluntary, and they have the rights to withdraw at any time. I addressed the risk factors associated with the study in the consent form. I also followed all ethical guidelines before the data collection process and after IRB approval of the consent form. An informed consent form was obtained before the beginning of the interview, and participants were given enough time to read and sign the consent form.

To maintain ethical concerns, a consent form, which included disclosure of risk and benefits associated with the study, and pseudonyms were used to maintain participants' confidentiality. Given the nature of the study, participants were informed that the information would remain confidential. All participants where be informed that the study is voluntary and there would be no coercion to participate in the study. The participants were given the opportunity to relax during the interviews, and with an understanding that they can discontinue the interview at any time. In addition, because this study was conducted outside the United States, the IRB guidelines were upheld. The IRB guidelines indicated that researchers consult with the international compilation of regulations provided by the USA Federal Office of Human Research Protections (OHRR). Therefore, the permission to conduct this study was obtained from the Office of the Sierra Leone Ethics and Scientific Review Committee Ministry of Health and Sanitation in Freetown, Sierra Leone located at Youiyi Building, Fifth Floor, East Wing. Walden University IRB indicated that applications for ethical behavior related to data collection in the US also applies to international countries. However, if the ethical standard of the international countries is stricter than those from the United States, then researchers can use the US ethical guidelines. In Sierra Leone, English is the official language, and all the participants in the study speak fluent English. Therefore, there was no language barrier associated with the study.

The treatment of all data was confidential. The data was collected upon the approval from IRB. This study took me two months to collect data, and 45 minutes of recorded interview with each participant. In addition, I took fieldnotes as I interviewed, and recorded the impression of participants' experiences, thoughts, and feelings. I scheduled a follow-up interview in case participants had additional questions. Participants that wanted to withdraw from the study were given the opportunity to leave without any repercussion.

The protection of data is an important aspect in research. Morse (2006) postulated that developing a plan to store and file data is an important aspect of data analysis. This study used hardcopies of interviews, as well as electronic copies of the interviews to store data. Electronic copies were stored on computer hard drive and flash drive. The participants' information was kept confidential at all times. Creswell (2009) recommended the use of hard copy files as a backup for all electronics files. I intended to destroy all data in 5years. Other confidential information such as field notes, informed consent, etc. were securely kept in a safe at my house. I was the only one with access to the data. According to Morse, mishandling of any data can compromise the outcome of the study. Other ethical issues such as conflict of interest or power differential and incentives were addressed before the beginning of the study. Therefore, there was no conflict of interest in doing this study. All participants were informed that there would be no compensation for participating in this study.

Summary

Chapter 3 provided information of the research methodology that was used in the study and the other aspects of the methodology. Chapter 3 also includes a rationale for choosing a qualitative phenomenological research design; plans for sampling data collection, and analysis for participants' protections, and issues related to trustworthiness. The procedures used in selecting participants, sampling strategies, instrument and how the data was analyzed were outlined in this section. Chapter 4 presents the results of the analysis of the interview data collection, data coding, and a description of the findings.

CHAPTER 4

Result

Introduction

The purpose of this study was to explore HCWs' perspectives about their mental health while providing care to Ebola patients. Participants were asked interview questions designed to address the following research questions:

>RQ1. How do HCWs in Freetown, Sierra Leone describe their lived experiences regarding their own mental health when treating patients with Ebola virus disease?

>RQ2. How do HCWs feel about their abilities to cope with stress while treating patients with the Ebola virus disease?

>RQ3. How do HCWs describe their lived experiences of the mental health care treatment they received while treating patients with the Ebola virus disease?

Chapter 4 includes the interview analysis for the study. This chapter also addresses the setting of the study, demographics, data collection, data analysis, and evidence of trustworthiness, concluding with a summary. This study enabled HCWs to voice their opinions on their own mental health while providing care to highly infectious patients.

Setting of the Study

I conducted all interviews in a café outside of Connaught Hospital at 6 Lamina Sankoh Street in Freetown, Sierra Leone. Ten participants were interviewed onsite. The weather was sunny during all of the interviews. There was no personal or organizational condition that influenced participants or the result of the study. The interviews were conducted on participants' own time (nonworking hours) and on different dates.

Demographics

Table 1 provides information about the participants' demographics. Participants' ages ranged from 36 to 60 years. All participants were in the healthcare field (nine nurses and one medical doctor); see Figure 1. Participants' educational backgrounds ranged from high school education to university level. Participants were from six different tribes (Mende, Temne, Limba, Kono, Mandingo, and Fuller); see Figure 2. All of the participants spoke English fluently. In addition, eight participants were married, and two were unmarried.

Table 1
Demographics of the Participants

Gender	Age	Education	Marital status
P1 (male)	36	University	Married
P2 (female)	47	College	Married
P3 (female)	44	College	Married
P4 (male)	39	Graduate	Married
P5 (male)	48	High school	Married
P6 (male)	58	High school	Married
P7 (male)	56	College	Married
P8 (male)	60	High school	Married
P9 (male)	57	College	Unmarried
P10 (male)	43	College	Unmarried

Note. P=Participant.

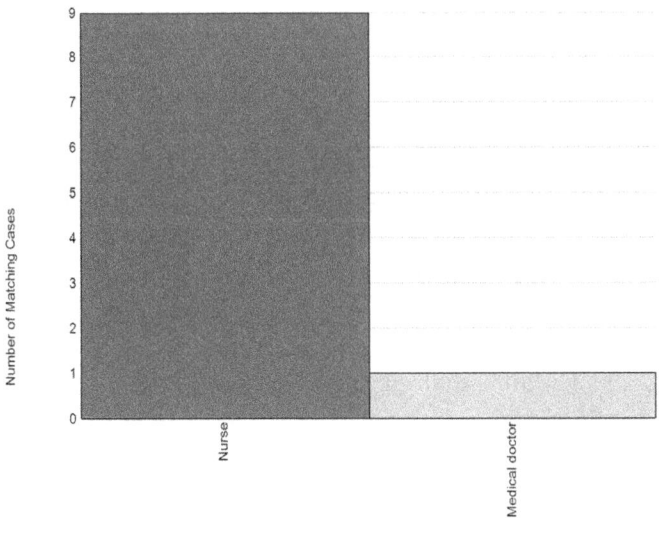

Figure 1. Health care workers' occupations—Cases by attribute value.

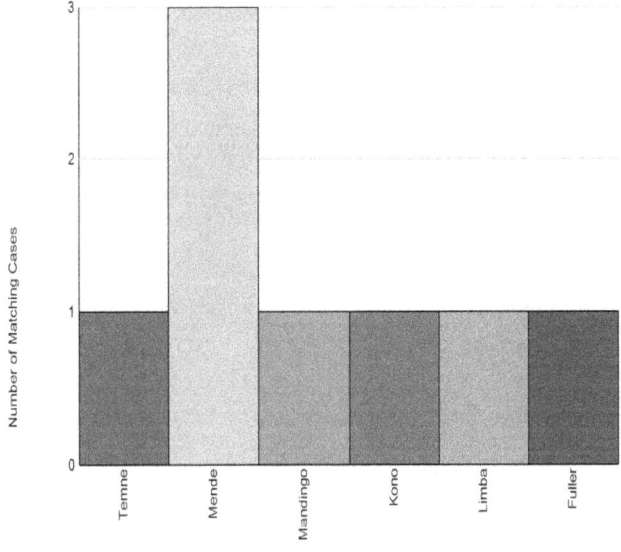

Figure 2. Health care workers' tribes—Cases by attribute value.

Data Collection

Data were collected from 10 participants in a café outside of Connaught Hospital at 6 Lamina Sankoh Street in Freetown, Sierra Leone. Participants were recruited by posting flyers. To answer the research questions, each participant was asked a series of semi structured questions. Each participant was encouraged to read the invitation letter and consent form before signing them, as proposed in Chapter 3. In addition, participants were informed that the interview would be audiotaped and that I would be taking field notes during the interviews. I also informed all participants that they could withdraw from the study at any time. All participants signed the consent form before the start of the interview.

I interviewed participants separately, and the interview process went on without any problem, as participants appeared calm and comfortable. Each interview lasted for no more than 45 minutes. I used an interview guide protocol (see Appendix B) to enable participants to elaborate on their lived experiences. The interview guide protocol reminded me of the questions to ask. As such, it enabled me to stay focused on the topic. My time was managed efficiently by using the interview guide questions. Probing questions during the interviews gave participants the opportunity to provide in-depth information. I also used probes to prompt participants to provide full narratives of their lived experiences when providing care for Ebola virus patients. On the first day, two participants were interviewed at different times; on the second day, two participants were interviewed at different times; on the third day, two participants were interviewed at different times; on the fourth day, three participants were interviewed at different times; and on the fifth day, one participant was interviewed at 5:30 p.m. I used my computer and flash drive to file audiotapes and field notes for the interviews. All data collected were stored in a safe location under lock and key at my house. This approach protected the participants in this study. There was no variation from the data collection plan presented in Chapter 3. There was no unusual circumstance encountered.

Data Analysis

NVivo 10 enabled me to manage the data and generate findings from the data. Data coding and analysis were completed to answer the research questions. Coding is an iterative, analytical process in which data are organized, sorted, and categorized for analysis. Codes capture the essence of a research story, and when clustered together as patterns, they actively facilitate the development of categories and their connections (Saldaña, 2015). They are tags and labels for assigning units of meaning to the descriptive or inferential information compiled during a study (Erickson, 2012).

Open coding was used to look for distinct concepts and the data to develop first- level categories, as well as second- (third-, fourth-, etc.) level codes that were associated and coded to the primary codes. At the first level of coding, I looked for distinct concepts in the data to form the basic categories or units of analysis. Three rounds of coding were done.

In Round 1 coding, three transcripts were imported into NVivo for coding, which represented the first-level codes named RQ1, RQ2, and RQ3. The second-level codes were generated based on the research questions and coding of the transcripts. The names of the codes were assigned directly for the words that comprised each interview question, and answers in the transcripts were directly aligned to the appropriate first-level codes to ensure consistency. For example, participants were asked about their mental health while providing care to Ebola patients. Participants discussed various mental illness symptoms that they experienced. The code for these coded passages of the text was mental illness symptoms (see Tables 2-4).

In the second round of coding, each transcript was reopened, and open coding was conducted again. The coding labels were assigned using NVivo codes or words that participants stated in the interviews. The codes or labels were developed directly from a word, words, or phrases from the coded passages of text. The data were coded and grouped according to similarities. For example, one answer that participants gave to the question about coping with stress was that they believed in their faith. The NVivo code assigned to these passages of the text was spirituality (see Tables 2-4).

In the third round of coding, a thorough review of the coding was carried out to ensure that NVivo codes had been assigned properly and to collapse any closely similar codes together.

The codes were as follows:

- Depression
- Anxiety
- Sleepless nights
- Shaking
- Chills
- Sickness
- Fast heartbeat
- Joint pain
- Sweating
- Flashbacks
- Choking
- Headaches
- Panic attack
- Weight loss
- Lack of gov support
- Lack of medication_ psychotropic drugs
- Lack of psychological help
- Poor quality
- Psychologists not good
- More focus on medical
- Professional counseling not adequate
- Lack of planning
- Death
- No one cares
- Racing thoughts
- Fear of unknown
- Embarrassment
- Fear of being called crazy
- A nightmare
- Panic
- Over vigilance
- Intrusive
- Love being HCW
- Suicidal

- Mental illness not taken seriously
- Spirituality
- Prayer
- Counseling by pastor
- Read Bible
- Deep breathing
- Drinking
- Meditation
- Family issues
- Problems at work
- HCWs did not discuss problem
- Reliving experience
- Cannot escape thoughts
- Life is different
- Not taking care of self
- Mental breakdown
- Faced discrimination
- Psychological help
- Awareness
- Medication
- Gov standards to fight depression
- Funding for mental health
- God
- Spiritual guidance
- Faith
- Controlling my thoughts
- Being strong for patients
- Psychotherapy
- Lack of coping mechanisms
- Lack of funding
- Emotional issues
- Crying
- Hopelessness
- Frustration
- Unable to cope with stress
- Could not perform work effectively
- Came close to death
- Life is a mess
- Treatment ineffective

- Costly
- Unaffordable treatment
- Lack of qualified mental health
- Medications ineffective
- Undiagnosed mental illness
- Gov support inadequate
- Mental health system inadequate
- Clinics lacking resources
- Mental health educ
- Effective mental health treatment
- Affordable mental health treatment
- Use of native herbs
- Medicines
- Qualified mental health professionals

Themes Development

Nine emergent patterns were identified from the data based on the analysis: four from research question 1, three from research question 2, and two from research question 3. The themes are listed below.

Research Question 1:

- Mental Illness Symptoms
- Personal Thoughts and Feelings
- Strategies for Coping
- Detrimental Impacts

Research Question 2:

- Coping with Stress
- Personal Consequences of Inadequate Mental Health Treatment
- Shortfalls in the Mental Health System

Research Question 3:

- Problems with Mental Health Care
- Recommendations to Improve Mental Health Treatment

Discrepant Cases

There was no discrepant case to report because my findings are not incompatible with the literature review on Chapter 2.

Evidence of Trustworthiness

Credibility

Credibility in this study was accomplished by allowing participants to listen to their own interview questions. The strategy used to maintain credibility was member checking. Participants had the opportunity to clarify responses. This study captured a clear picture of HCWs' perspective on their mental health while providing care to Ebola patients in Freetown, Sierra Leone. As a qualitative researcher, I upheld a nonbiased approach to ensure that my experience did not interfere with the interview process. This approach was accomplished by being objective through the interview process. The researcher proceeded with data collection until saturation was accomplished (Creswell, 2009).

Transferability

To ensure transferability, a full description of the main participants was used as a guide to ensure that the findings could be applied to other population (Denzin &Lincoln, 1994). In addition, the result from the study would remain available to other researchers studying the same or similar population.

Dependability

Dependability was accomplished as the result would enable other researchers to use my study for research purposes, as indicated in my data analysis plan. The result of the interview questions was recorded and reported in detail. The transcripts, codes, and themes were kept in a safe location to enable other researchers to use for future research purposes. All data will be destroyed in five years after the completion of this study.

Confirmability

The research findings brought a unique perspective that was supported by my data collection during the interview process. To enforce conformability, I employed a nonbiased approach during the research process. A nonbiased approach was important because I was born in Freetown, Sierra Leone, as I could have easily brought my personal bias to this study. It is important the result of the study be accepted and utilized by other researchers. I provided a full detailed explanation of all the necessary steps taken in the study and how I reached the final decision. To maintain confirmability, my role and position as a researcher, and how the data would be gathered were provided to participants. At the end of the study, I conducted a final review to ensure that the study was properly done, as indicated in Chapter 3.

Results

I was able to understand and transcribed participants' spoken words verbatim. Findings from data analysis indicated that HCWs who treated Ebola patients experienced mental health symptoms during 2014and2015 Ebola outbreak in Freetown, Sierra Leone. Participants also elaborated on the need for effective mental health treatment and other strategies for coping with mental illness. The majority of the participants stated that they were unable to cope with the stress factors associated with the Ebola outbreak.

Discrepant Cases

There was no discrepant case that contributes to an emerging pattern of the finding. It is imperative to recognize discrepant cases because they represent cases that do not belong to the emerging patterns of evidence. According to Patton (2002), discrepant cases create barriers around emerging patterns that can change the primary pattern of findings.

Research Question 1

How do HCWs in Freetown, Sierra Leone describe their lived experiences regarding their own mental health when treating Ebola patients? The answer provided by participants during the interviews showed that participants experienced mental illness symptoms. During the data collection, I was able to ask additional questions to enable participants to elaborate on their perceptions of their lived experiences. The first semi- structured interview question that was used to address *RQ1* was–Describe for me your mental health when treating patients with the Ebola virus disease? This question was asked to get participants to provide a full narrative of their mental health (Creswell, 2009; Patton, 2002) when treating patients with Ebola virus disease. Themes emerged from this question were mental illness symptoms, personal thoughts, and feelings, strategies for coping, detrimental impacts (See Table 2), The majority of the participants experience anxiety and depression. For example, Participant 1 stated, "I went into severe anxiety." Participant 2 stated, "I became depressed because of the isolation." Other participants complained of other symptoms such as shaky feelings, intrusive thoughts, and over vigilance. For instance, Participant 5 stated, "I was shaking like a leaf and I was having bad thoughts in my head."

Table 2

Themes and Codes Related to HCWs' Mental Health

Research questions	Themes	Codes	Aggregate references
RQ1: How do HCWs in Sierra Leone describe their lived experiences regarding their own mental health when treating patients with the Ebolavirus?	Mental illness symptoms	Depression, anxiety, sleepless nights shaking, chills, sickness, fast heartbeat, joint pain, sweating, flashbacks, choking, headaches, panic attack, weight loss, racing thoughts	50

Personal thoughts and feelings	Death, no one cares, fear of unknown embarrassment, fear of being called crazy, denial, a nightmare, panic, over vigilance, _intrusive, love being HCW, suicidal, mental illness not taken seriously	25
Strategies for coping	Spirituality, prayer, counseling by pastors read Bible, deep breathing, drinking, meditation	27
Detrimental impacts	Family issues, problems at work, HCWs did not discuss problems, reliving experience, cannot escape thoughts, life is different, not taking care of self, drinking, mental breakdown, faced discrimination	18

Research Question 2

How do HCWs feel about their abilities to cope with stress while treating patients with the Ebola virus disease? The answers provided by participants during the interview showed that the majority of HCWs were unable to cope with stress while treating patients with the Ebola virus disease. For instance, Participant 3 stated, "I did not know how to cope with stress!" Participant 8 stated, "I used my Bible to cope with stress!"

In addition, I used a second interview question to addressed *RQ2*. Participants were asked – Talk to me about how you responded or coped with the death of your patients, friends, or family member? This question enabled participants to reflect on their coping skills while providing care to Ebola patients. Themes emerged from this question were (a) coping with stress, (b) shortfalls in the mental health system, and (c) personal consequences of inadequate mental health treatment (See Table 3). While participants 2, 8, 9, and 10 indicated they used spirituality to cope with stress, the majority of the participants indicated that they were unable to cope with stress during the Ebola outbreak. For instance, Participant 3 indicated, "I felt a sense of hopelessness and I was unable to cope." Participant 4 stated, "there were no coping measures." And, Participant 5 stated, "I did not know how to cope." Other participants, such as participant 9 and 10 blamed the government for not providing an effective measure to cope with the Ebola outbreak. Participants 1 and 5 stated that they could have coped if they were exposed to adequate mental health treatments.

Table 3
Themes and Codes Related to HCWs' Coping

Research questions	Themes	Codes	Aggregate references
RQ2. How do HCWs feel about their abilities to cope with stress while treating patients with the Ebola virus disease?	Coping with stress	Spirituality, prayer, God, spiritual guidance, faith, controlling my thoughts, being strong for patients, psychotherapy	15
	Shortfalls in the mental health system	Lack of government support, lack of coping mechanisms, lack of funding, lack of medicine	18
	Personal consequences of inadequate mental health treatment	Emotional issues, depressed, far, crying hopelessness, frustration, unable to cope with stress, could not perform work effectively, came close to death, life is a mess	17

Research Question 3

How do HCWs describe their lived experiences of the mental health care they received while treating patients with Ebola virus disease? The answer provided by the majority of the participants during the interview indicated that they did not receive adequate mental health treatment. Themes emerged from this question were problems with mental health care and resources and recommendation to improve mental health treatment (See Table 4). Participant 2 stated, "I received psychotropic medications for mental illness symptoms, but they were ineffective." Participant 8 stated, "The psychotropic medications given to HCWs were ineffective or placebo." Participant 9 stated, "The mental health treatment was bad, not good." Participant 10 stated, "The medication given to me did not help me." All participants recommended that the government promote effective mental health treatment for healthcare workers. Participants also recommended education on the signs and symptoms of mental illness. Further, Participant 3 stated, "The government should start using natural herbs to treat mental illness symptoms."

Table 4

Themes and Codes Related to HCWs' Treatment

Research questions	Themes	Codes	Aggregate references
RQ3. How do HCWs describe their lived experiences of the mental health care they received while treating patients with Ebola virus disease?	Problems with mental health care	Treatment ineffective, costly unaffordable treatment, lack of qualified mental health, medications ineffective, undiagnosed mental illness, gov support inadequate, mental health system inadequate, clinics lacking resources, lack of gov support, lack of medication_ psychotropic drugs, lack of psychological help, poor quality, psychologists not good, more focus on medical, professional counseling not adequate, lack of planning.	33

Needed resources and recommendations	Psychological help, awareness medication, gov standards to fight depression, funding for mental health, mental health educ, effective mental health treatment, affordable mental health treatment, use of native herbs	33

Summary

The purpose of this chapter was to write out the analysis of the research questions and provide detailed information about participants' experiences with their mental health while taking care of Ebola patients. There were 10 participants selected for the study. Participants were selected at Connaught hospital in Freetown, Sierra Leone. HCWs who provided care to Ebola patients were directly included in the study. In other to gain a deeper and in-depth understanding of the experiences of HCWs in Freetown, Sierra Leone about their mental health while providing care to Ebola patient; three research questions were designed.

The first research question was designed to capture the overall perspective of healthcare workers lived experiences of their own mental health while treating Ebola patients. It was evident from their explanations that they suffered mental illness symptoms. Major themes that emerged from this research question were mental illness symptoms, personal thoughts and feelings, strategies for coping, and detrimental impacts. Participant responses from this research question verified that HCWs experienced anxiety, depression, nightmares, suicidal thoughts, panic attacks, insomnia, and sleepless nights etc.

The second research question was designed to capture how do HCWs feel about their abilities to cope with stress while providing care to Ebola patients. The major themes that emerged from this research question were coping with stress, shortfalls in the mental health system, and personal consequences of inadequate mental health treatment. In response to this research question, the majority of the participants indicated that they were unable to cope with stress while taking care of Ebola patients. These feelings were shared by six of the participants. The majority of the HCWs perceptions toward coping with stress, especially during the Ebola outbreak, was that they were unable to cope, especially when they watched their patients die.

The third research question was designed to explore the lived experiences of mental health care treatment HCWs received while providing treatment to Ebola patients. Themes derived from this question were problems with mental health care and recommendations to improve mental health treatment. All the participants gave similar responses that the mental health treatment provided to them was inadequate and ineffective. Participants were concerned that the lack of effective treatment enabled them to have difficulties to cope with stress during the Ebola outbreak.

Also, participants felt that the government needs to be more involved with helping all Sierra Leoneans with mental illness. Participants felt that most of the people in Sierra Leone are ashamed of being labeled mentally ill. Therefore, education was referenced by most of the participant as an effective way to promote mental health awareness. Participants were concerned that many people with mental illness cannot afford effective mental health treatment. As a result, participants are encouraging the government to advocate for affordable mental health treatment for all Sierra Leoneans. Majority of the participants urged the government to develop effective coping measures for healthcare workers during an epidemic.

While Chapter 4 provided the analysis of the research questions and provided detailed information about participants' experiences of their own mental health, Chapter 5 provided an overview of why the study was conducted. Chapter 5 also highlights the interpretation, finding, and limitation of the study. Recommendation and positive social change were also addressed.

CHAPTER 5

Discussion, Recommendations, and Conclusions

Introduction

The purpose of this phenomenological study was to explore HCWs' perspectives on their mental health while working with Ebola patients. HCWs were asked to describe their lived experiences while treating patients with EVD. Ten participants were selected from one geographical location in Freetown, Sierra Leone. Participants were interviewed outside Connaught Hospital.

I only selected HCWs who had worked directly with Ebola patients. Participants were asked to provide their perceptions pertaining to three research questions. The first research question was as follows: How do HCWs in Freetown, Sierra Leone describe their lived experiences regarding their own mental health when treating patients with Ebola virus disease? The second research question was the following: How do HCWs feel about their abilities to cope with stress while treating patients with the Ebola virus disease? The third research question was as follows: How do HCWs describe their lived experiences of the mental health care treatment they received while treating patients with the Ebola virus disease?

The findings of this study were compared to the literature reviewed In Chapter 2. I expect that the study will benefit healthcare professionals and ordinary Sierra Leoneans with mental illness. The findings were also interpreted in the context of the stress process model and hermeneutic phenomenology.

Pearlin et al.'s (1981) stress process model was selected as a lens to analyze the findings of this study. The stress process model is helpful in understanding the stress factors associated with HCWs during an epidemic. Hermeneutic phenomenology was used as a lens to analyze the findings of this study. Hermeneutic phenomenology enables researchersto understand the lived experiences of a person or a group. As I proceeded with this study, several major themes were identified from three research questions. Major themes were selected based on the similarity of meaning of words and phrases. In addition, limitations of the study, recommendations, implications of the study and the conclusion of the study are discussed in this chapter.

Key Findings

This section summarizes the key findings from the themes for each research question. Mental illness symptoms, personal thoughts and feelings, strategies for coping, and detrimental impact were the major themes that emerged from *Research Question 1*. All of the participants complained of either depression, anxiety, or PTSD, and they were afraid of being called crazy. Although a few participants used the Bible to cope with their mental illness symptoms, the majority of participants believed that they were unable to cope and that they faced discrimination after the Ebola outbreak. Three emergent patterns—coping with stress, shortfalls in the mental health system, and personal consequences of inadequate mental health treatment—were identified in relation to *Research Question 2*. The majority of the participants felt that they were unable to cope with stress while providing treatment to Ebola patients and blamed the government for not providing adequate measures to cope. Moreover, two emergent patterns—problems with mental health care and the need for resources and recommendations—were identified in relation to *Research Question 3*. Though participants stated that they received psychotropic medications while providing treatment to Ebola patients, they also noted that the psychotropic medications were not helpful. The nine major themes developed from data analysis were as follows:

- *Mental illness symptoms*: Participants complained of anxiety, depression, PTSD, and other psychological difficulties.
- *Personal thoughts and feelings*: Participants gave their opinions on the mental illness symptoms they experienced, the mental health system, and what could be done.
- *Strategies of coping*: Participants claimed that they used spirituality to cope; however, the majority of the participants stated that they were unable to cope.
- *Detrimental impacts*: Participants claimed that they were still suffering from the symptoms of mental illness and discrimination.
- *Coping with stress*: The majority of the participants claimed that they were unable to cope with stress.
- *Shortfalls in the mental health system*: Most of the participants claimed that the clinicians were not qualified and that mental health clinics lacked resources.
- *Personal consequences of inadequate mental health treatment*: Participants claimed that they would have coped if adequate treatments had been provided.
- *Problems with mental health care*: Participants claimed that there were problems with mental health care.
- *Recommendations to improve mental health treatments*: Participants gave recommendations on how to improve the mental health care system.

Interpretation of Findings

Extended Knowledge

The stress process model and hermeneutic phenomenology have never been used to explore the mental health of HCWs who provided treatments to Ebola patients. The result of the study adds to the body of knowledge on HCWs experiencing high stress that leads to mental illness symptoms. HCWs' sincere ignorance of mental illness symptoms because of lack of proper education, lack of effective mental health treatment, and inadequate resources contributes to increased mental health symptoms in this population.

Literature and Research Question 1 Findings

RQ1. How do HCWs in Freetown, Sierra Leone describe their lived experiences regarding their own mental health when treating patients with Ebola virus disease?

Ebola is a deadly disease that can affect the mental health of HCWs. Participants felt that they experienced symptoms of mental illness when treating patients with the Ebola virus. Participants complained of restlessness, fear, and difficulties sleeping at night. One of the symptoms elaborated by most participants was excessive worry that they were going to die. According to the DSM-V (APA, 2013), one of the common signs of anxiety is excessive worry. The DSM-V also indicates that sleep disturbance is often reported by people experiencing anxiety disorders. I noted that all participants complained about symptoms of mental illness during the Ebola outbreak. They also indicated that they were still experiencing these symptoms daily at the time of the study and that they were having difficulties in providing effective treatment to their patients. They stated that one of the causes of the symptoms they experienced was the stress they experienced during the Ebola outbreak. The DSM-V indicates that people with anxiety disorders exhibit difficulties in responding to stress. Similarly, Li et al. (2015) and Shoji et al. (2014) found that some of the emotional difficulties experienced by HCWs are anxiety and PTSD.

Furthermore, the perceptions of all the participants indicated that they were depressed. Participants believed that they experienced sadness, feelings of hopelessness, loss of interest, insomnia, suicidal ideation, and tiredness. I noted that the sudden outbreak of the Ebola virus produced stress for HCWs while working with Ebola patients. Pearlin (1989) postulated that stressors may be both internal and external, with external factors involving the individual's immediate environment. All participants stated that the sudden change of environment with the Ebola outbreak increased their stress level, which caused them to be depressed. All participants believed that the focus was on finding a way to eradicate the Ebola virus and not on their own mental health.

Existing literature indicates that during epidemics, HCWs (nurses, doctors, and emergency room technicians) experience anxiety, depression, and PTSD (Li et al., 2015; Shoji et al., 2014). My study found that some HCWs (nurses and doctors) who cared for Ebola patients used spirituality to cope with their mental illness symptoms. This finding adds to the body of knowledge.

Participants in my study mentioned that they did not get adequate mental health treatment during the Ebola virus outbreak. They reported that even though they received some teaching on coping skills from healthcare professionals, it was not enough for them. They believed that the government should work with qualified mental health professionals to provide adequate mental health treatment for all Sierra Leoneans. HCWs complained that psychotropic drugs were ineffective and clinicians were not good. All participants blamed the government for not doing enough to support their mental health while they provided treatment to Ebola patients. Besides their own mental health, participants believed that the government should focus on effective mental health treatment for all Sierra Leoneans for future epidemics.

HCWs are vulnerable to stress, which can lead to mental illness. In their study, Myers (1994) and Radeke and Mahoney (2000) indicated that HCWs (nurses) experienced increased anxiety, depression, and mental fatigue. Myers and Radeke and Mahoney found in their research that HCWs (nurses) who were vulnerable to stress were given the opportunity to use mindfulness-based stress reduction (MBSR) to cope with their stress. In contrast, participants in my study were not given the opportunity to use MBSR to cope with their stress while providing care to Ebola patients. Participants in my study perceivedthe mental healthcare system of Sierra Leone as ineffective. According to Jalloh et al. (2018) and Scott et al. (2009), there is compelling evidence that HCWs (nurses and medical doctors) experience psychological stress and should be given high- quality mental health treatment. Similarly, in my study, HCWs who cared for Ebola patients complained of psychological stress and were seeking high-quality mental health care. The findings from the studies of Jalloh et al. and Scott et al. give credence to my findings. Lack of adequate mental health treatment for HCWs in Sierra Leone can affect the quality of work they provide to their patients and their activities of daily living.

Participants complained that the mental health symptoms they experienced prevented them from providing adequate treatment to their patients. Koinis et al. (2015) argued that symptoms of mental illness can affect the quality of services provided by HCWs (nurses). They also stated that if the psychological problems of HCWs are not taken seriously in West Africa, HCWs will have difficulties in providing quality care to their patients. Additionally, WHO (2016) called for adequate mental health treatment for HCWs (nurses and medical doctors) in the West African region after uncovering that HCWs were experiencing mental health difficulties.

The overall findings support the literature review's indication that HCWs should receive mental health treatment, especially when they are under stress. The findings also give credence to the notion that HCWs are vulnerable to high levels of stress at their workplace. These studies found that HCWs' mental health cannot be ignored. The overall perceptions of participants were that HCWs experienced mental health symptoms while providing care to Ebola patients.

Literature and Research Question 2 Findings

> RQ2. How do HCWs feel about their abilities to cope with stress while treating patients with the Ebola virus disease?

The themes derived from this research question were coping with stress, shortfalls in the mental health system, and personal consequences of inadequate mental health treatment.

Four out of 10participants believed that they coped well with the Ebola outbreak while treating patients with Ebola virus. These participants felt that their religious beliefs and controlling their thoughts helped them to cope while treating patients with Ebola virus. Participant 8 contended that he was able to cope because of his love for his work. Though these participants were able to cope, they also recommended that the government provide effective psychotherapy for HCWs. In their study, Koh et al. (2015) found that HCWs who had coping skills complained less of psychological morbidity and burnout. Petrites et al. (2016) reported in their study that 72% of HCWs in West Africa used religion to cope with the loss of their clients. The findings of this study may encourage HCWs and mental health care professionals to change their attitudes toward the mental health system in Sierra Leone. Khalid et al. (2016) found in their study that the two factors that helped HCWs cope during an epidemic were positive attitudes and strict precautions derived from safety standards. These findings are in alignment with my study, as this study encourages a positive attitude in coping with an epidemic.

Furthermore, six out of 10 participants felt that they were unable to cope with the Ebola outbreak while providing care to Ebola patients. In their study, Jordan et al. (2016) reported that the majority of HCWs have difficulties in coping with stress. Participants claimed that their stress levels were too high, which affected their coping abilities. Fernandes and Nirmala (2017) reported that high stress levels among HCWs contributed to emotional burnout. The majority of the participants in my study stated that when they saw their patients die, they were unable to cope. WHO (2015) has encouraged public officials to provide adequate coping-related mental health services for Sierra Leoneans. Some participants from my study responded that if some Sierra Leoneans had been educated on mental illness, they would have been able to cope with the symptoms of mental illness.

The WHO (2016) and CDC (2015) reported that HCWs in the West African region experienced high stress because of inadequate resources and poor living conditions. In my study, participants responded that adequate resources would enable them to cope better with high stress levels. A similar finding was shared by participants in a study, as they indicated that they were able to cope with an epidemic while taking care of their patients (Khalid et al., 2016). This finding gives credence to Betancourt et al.'s (2016) finding. Betancourt et al. indicated that the government is the primary influence on HCWs' psychological well-being. Betancourt et al.'s finding was confirmed by Greenberg et al. (2015), who encouraged the development of adequate mental health care services for HCWs in Sierra Leone. A similar recommendation was given by deMenil et al. (2014), who stated that HCWs who were provided adequate mental health care at their workplace reported a reduction of their psychological symptoms. This finding was confirmed by Li et al. (2015), who indicated that adequate mental health care for HCWs in the Western Africa region would enable them to cope with stress. My study adds to the body of knowledge indicating that the personal consequences of inadequate mental health treatment for HCWs during an epidemic lead to mental health difficulties for them.

Literature and Research Question 3 Findings

> RQ3. How do HCWs describe their lived experiences of the mental health care treatment they received while treating patients with the Ebola virus disease?

The themes derived from this research question were problems with mental health care and needed resources and recommendations. While few participants mentioned that they received some treatment, all participants felt that their treatments were inadequate and ineffective. This report is supported by other findings in the literature review (Betancourt et al. 2016; CDC, 2015; Greenberg et al., 2015; WHO, 2016). Betancourt et al.; Greenberg; and WHO stressed the importance of adequate mental health care, adequate resources, and early diagnosis of mental illness for HCWs. Greenberg concluded that these aspects are relevant to providing adequate mental health care for Sierra Leoneans.

Participants felt that government officials had failed to implement a proper protocol that would help to combat mental illness. Some participants stated that the medications provided to them were expired. They responded that the doctors were unsure how to treat their psychological problems. Participants also mentioned that the clinicians were unqualified to help them with their psychological problems.

Another theme that emerged from *Research Question 3* was the recommendation to improve mental health treatment. Some participants believed that it is important to educate the public on mental illness. Participants stated that doctors could not just give medications to their patients, arguing that doctors must also educate their clients about mental illness. According to participants, most Sierra Leoneans do not want to seek mental health treatment because of stigmatization. Participants felt that most Sierra Leoneans do not know that they have mental illness and are diagnosed when it is too late. A study conducted by Padayacheya et al. (2017) reported that early mental health diagnosis is better than late diagnosis. Participants felt that lack of affordability is one of the reasons that mental illness is not diagnosed early. Lund et al. (2013) found in their study that mental illness is a major economic disadvantage for low-income populations in Africa. They recommended government assistance for low-income individuals in West Africa. deMenilal (2014) found that mental health costs in Africa are funded by private health insurance companies that only benefit the privileged.

This finding gives credence to a study conducted by Brolin Ribacke et al. (2016) that the mental health care system in Sierra Leone, West Africa was deplorable during the Ebola outbreak. This perspective was elaborated by all participants in my study. Above all, the participants indicated that adequate mental health care is expensive. WHO (2016) has stated that funding of adequate mental health care in the West African region remains extremely poor.

Some participants blamed the ignorance of the ordinary Sierra Leoneans for inadequate mental health treatment. They felt that if the majority of the people were educated, they would have advocated for adequate mental health care in Sierra Leone. Jalloh et al. (2018) found that sincere ignorance is one of the barriers to adequate mental health treatment in the West African region. Participants also maintained that free mental health care should be made available to all healthcare workers. The findings confirmed that there were problems with the mental health care HCWs received while providing treatments to Ebola patients. Therefore, HCWs gave recommendations on how to improve the mental healthcare system in Sierra Leone.

Theoretical Framework

The stress process model asserts that three factors describe the stressors individuals experience. These factors are stressors, motivation or mediations, and stress outcomes (Pearlin et al., 1981). Pearlin et al.'s stress process model was used as a lens of analysis to help understand HCWs' perspectives on their own mental health while providing care to Ebola patients. This theory was also chosen as a theoretical framework. All participants in the study responded that they experienced mental illness symptoms while providing treatment to Ebola patients.

Pearlin et al.'s (1981) stress process model enabled me to understand the stressors HCWs experienced while providing care to EVD patients. This theory facilitates the understanding of how different stressors foster mental illness. HCWs who participated in this study during the Ebola epidemic did not expect the sudden outbreak of the Ebola virus. Pearlin postulated that there are two categories of stressors: event stressors and chronic stressors. According to Pearlin, event stressors happen unexpectedly. Therefore, the 2014 Ebola outbreak can be categorized as event stressor. On the other hand, chronic stressors involved different kinds of strains. An example of chronic stressor experienced by HCWs during the Ebola outbreak was a status strain. Pearlin (1999) postulated that status strain involves an individual's social and hierarchical structure. In the context of HCWs during the EVD outbreak, an obvious example of this stressor was the lack of mental health funding in West Africa, which affected mental health services. This issue caused individuals in this population to be susceptible to an increased amount of stress.

HCWs during the EVD outbreak were exposed to stressors from different areas of their perceived roles, which created role conflict. According to Pearlin, role conflict increases a person's stress level. HCWs during the Ebola outbreak simultaneously fulfilled their responsibilities at home and at work.

HCWs experienced psychological symptoms caused by the lack of resources to help them cope with their stress. According to the stress process model, the different psychological symptoms experienced by HCWs is called individual strain. On the other hand, the lack of resources and support is called environmental strains. Therefore, HCWs who provided treatment to Ebola patients experienced both kinds of strain.

All HCWs during the Ebola outbreak worked long hours to help their clients and did not get restful sleep. HCWs complained of psychological discomfort while providing care to Ebola patients. According to the stress process model, this kind of stressor is called quotidian strain. Therefore, HCWs who provided treatment to Ebola patients experienced quotidian strain.

Conceptual Framework

Hermeneutic phenomenology enabled me to understand the lived experiences of HCWs who cared for Ebola patients. HCWs were able to relay their lived experiences on their psychological discomfort, poor mental health treatment, and inadequate resources in Sierra

Leone. Hermeneutic phenomenological conceptual framework asserts that individuals can explain their ways of seeing things, knowing things, and the way things are related to them (Valandra, 2012). This framework facilitates the understanding of the symptoms of mental illness HCWs in Freetown, Sierra Leone experienced while providing treatment to Ebola patients.

The finding from this study shows that HCWs experienced both internal and external stressors. The Hermeneutic phenomenology gave me the opportunity to understand the lived experienced HCWs who provided treatments to Ebola patients. However, the stress process model provided insight into how HCWs handled stress while providing care to Ebola patients. From the internal and external stressors, the majority of the HCWs were unable to cope with the stressors while providing treatment to Ebola patients. HCWs were unable to cope with stress due to inadequate resources and the lack of effective coping measures.

From a general point of view, the stress process model was not only used as a lens of analysis, but it was selected to uncover other factors associated with the study. For example, other factors such as sincere ignorance and poor living conditions increased HCWs stress. These factors, intertwined with the stress process model, emphasized the importance of educating HCWs on effective coping measures to combat stress, especially during an epidemic.

Limitation of the Study

During the study, I was able to self-check on several issues. I was born in Freetown, Sierra Leone and participant responses made me uncomfortable. As a qualitative researcher, I had to remove myself from their experiences and remained more objective as participants told their lived experiences. Further, the study only included HCWs in the Westin area of Freetown, Sierra Leone and excluded HCWs in the provinces. Therefore, the study may not generalize to other areas of Sierra Leone, other countries, or HCWs treating other epidemics.

I was the sole data collector and there was no peer review during the interview session. The research findings may not be transferable to other populations. This study was limited to only 10 participants who worked directly with Ebola patients. Additional studies on this phenomenon could include HCWs lived experiences of their own mental health while providing care to Ebola patients from different geographical areas in the Western region of Africa.

Recommendations

This study only focused on HCWs' perspectives on their own mental health while providing treatment to Ebola patients in Freetown, Sierra Leone. The experiences of ordinary Sierra Leoneans on this phenomenon should be included in future studies in order to provide optimal measures to cope with mental illness in Freetown, Sierra Leone. This study only included HCWs that were fluent in English. The common language in Sierra Leone is Creole. Future study should include participants that are fluent in Creole to get a deeper understanding of this phenomenon. It is also my recommendation that mental health care professionals conduct yearly workshops to improve adequate mental healthcare in Sierra Leone. Mugisha et al. (2017) stated that there would be an increase in mental health problems among HCWs in West Africa if better strategies for adequate mental health care are not implemented. According to my findings, healthcare practitioners need to provide empirically based education on the effect of an epidemic on the mental health of the health practitioners. Such education should be a mandatory workshop for all healthcare workers. Education on mental illness as well as on the cure for Ebola virus, especially during an epidemic would enable HCWs to cope during an epidemic. I am recommending that the government implemented effective strategies, such as yearly workshops on mental illness to combat mental health crisis during an epidemic.

Implications

Positive Social Change

HCWs in Freetown, Sierra Leone were given the opportunity to voice their lived experiences on their own mental health while providing care for Ebola patients. HCWs with undiagnosed mental illness have difficulties adjusting to their everyday lives (WHO, 2016).

In fact, several studies have been conducted to help address the mental health problem in the West African region (Greenberg et al., 2015). However, as of yet, the mental health system in Freetown, Sierra Leone remains inadequate. On the level of individuals, the responses about mental health symptoms, coping and lack of treatment provided by HCWs in this study will affect positive social change. These findings would enable Sierra Leoneans, especially HCWs to understand the signs and symptoms of mental illness they may experience.

I will make the finding of the study available to the Ministry of Health and Sanitation in Sierra Leone so that they will have knowledge of the mental health concerns HCWs experienced during the Ebola outbreak. In addition, I will make myself reachable to healthcare professionals and government officials to discuss any relevant issues about the major findings of the study. Because it is my goal to affect positive social change, I will start a mental health clinic in Freetown, Sierra Leone after the completion of my degree. The purpose of this clinic will be to provide and promote effective mental health treatment to low income Sierra Leoneans. It is my hope that this study and the opening of my mental health clinic in Freetown, Sierra Leone would empower all Sierra Leoneans and bring positive social change.

Based on my findings, hopefully, government officials in Freetown, Sierra Leone would start the dialogue on effective mental health care for all Sierra Leoneans. Government officials and mental healthcare officials can access the findings by contacting me directly as I will make myself available via telephone, email, and website to discuss any relevant issues about the major findings of the study. This study found that the mental health treatment provided to HCWs in Freetown, Sierra Leone was inadequate and ineffective. Adequate mental health treatment for HCWs would enable them to provide adequate care to their patients (deMenil et al.,2014). In addition, I will encourage government officials to provide adequate education on mental health.

The result of the study will foster collaboration between mental health professionals and government officials to engage in effective communication about mental healthcare in Sierra Leone. Effective education takes place in collaboration (Vygotsky, 1978). This study shows that HCWs during the Ebola outbreak have serious concerns about their mental health. Further, the study provides relevant information that mental health care professionals would use to address the mental health problems in Sierra Leone. Participants were concerned that their mental health might decline if there is another Ebola outbreak. The result of the study is also important as it would enable government officials to understand the signs and symptoms of mental illness. It is imperative that government officials know that HCWs who provided treatment to Ebola patients experience mental health difficulties. The study also found that the lack of affordable cost for mental health is making it difficult for many Sierra Leoneans to seek adequate mental health care. Studies conducted by Lund et al. (2013) suggested that the government help cover the cost of mental health for low-income individuals in Africa.

HCWs involvement was an important factor in this study, as they are the most vulnerable to stress during an epidemic. HCWs are vulnerable to anxiety, depression, and PTSD (Li et al., 2015; Shoji et al., 2014). HCWs reported that they played multiple roles and were mostly affected by the Ebola epidemic. The result of the study might empower ordinary Sierra Leoneans to advocate for better mental healthcare.

Methodological and Theoretical Implications

The use of phenomenological approach coupled with Pearlin et al. (1981) stress process model and Heidegger (1889) hermeneutic phenomenology was appropriate for this study because this study was a qualitative study, an in-depth perspective was provided by participants. In addition, it can be appropriate for future researchers studying healthcare workers' perspectives on an epidemic, especially HCWs mental health during an Ebola virus outbreak. Pearlin's et al. stress process model and Heidegger's (1889) hermeneutic phenomenology are well designed to capture the needed data from participants about their mental illness during the Ebola outbreak.

Conclusion

As I conducted the study, I was aware that participants experienced mental illness but did not get adequate mental health care. The lack of adequate mental health care prompted participants to be frustrated and blame the government. This study was unique because it gave HCWs during the Ebola outbreak in Freetown, Sierra Leone the opportunity to talk about their lived experiences with mental illness. The finding of the study showed that the mental health care system in Sierra Leone is inadequate. And, as of yet, after the Ebola outbreak, the mental health of HCWs continues to be ignored. The study found that many in Freetown view mental illness as a stigma and even though they experienced signs and symptoms of mental illness they refused to seek help. This should not be the case for HCWs, because good mental health would enable HCWs to provide adequate care for their patients. Many Sierra Leoneans cannot afford adequate mental health care and therefore turn to their religion.

Finally, mental illness continues to affect the lives of many Sierra Leoneans. Mental health care professionals and the government are encouraged to advocate for adequate mental health care for all Sierra Leoneans. Mental illness is seen as a serious psychological problem and factors such as stress, poverty, inadequate resources, poor education, and lack of advocacy can promote the continuation of mental illness. Mental health officials have not done enough to combat mental illness in Sierra Leone. However, if mental health officials start the dialogue, government officials might join them to implement effective strategies to combat mental illness in Sierra Leone, especially during an epidemic.

References

Abendroth, M., & Flannery, J. (2006). Predicting the risk of compassion fatigue: A study of hospice nurses. *Journal of Hospice and Palliative Nursing, 8,* 346-356.

Alonso, P., Price, B., Conteh, A. R., Valle, C., Turay, P. E., Paton, L., &Turay, J. A. (2014). Where there is no psychiatrist: A mental health programme in Sierra Leone. *South African Journal of Obstetrics &Gynaecology, 20*(3), 88-93. doi:10.7196/SAJP.4

American Psychiatric Association.(2000). *Diagnostic and statistical manual of mental disorders* (4th ed., text rev.). Washington, DC: Author.

American Psychiatric Association. (2013). *Diagnostic and statistical manual of mentaldisorders* (5th ed.). Arlington, VA: American Psychiatric Publishing.

Aneshensel, C. S. (1992). Social stress: Theory and research. *AnnualReview of Sociology,18*(1), 15-38.

Ansumana, R., Keitell, S., Roberts, G. M., Ntoumi, F., Petersen, E., Ippolito, G., & Zumla, A. (2017). Impact of infectious disease epidemics on tuberculosis diagnostic, management, and prevention services: Experiences and lessons from the 2014–2015 Ebola virus disease outbreak in West Africa. *International Journal of Infectious Diseases,* 56101-56104. doi:10.1016/j.ijid.2016.10.010

Bangura, K. S., Lynch, K., &Binns, J. A. (2013). Coping with the impacts of weather changes in rural Sierra Leone. *International*

Journal of Sustainable Development & World Ecology, 20(1), 20-31. doi:10.1080/13504509.2012.740511

Barrera, I. (2011). An ecological systems theory approach in looking at mental healthcare barriers in the Latino community. Retrieved from http://www.amazon.com/ecological-systems-approach- barrierscommunity/dp/1243500077

Beavogui, A. H., Delamou, A., Yansane, M. L., Konde, M. K., Diallo, A. A., Aboulhab, J., ... Keita, S. (2016). Clinical research during the Ebola virus disease outbreak in Guinea: Lessons learned and ways forward. *Clinical Trials,13*(1), 73-78.

Beeching, N. J., Fenech, M., &Houlihan, C. F. (2014). Ebola virus disease. *BMJ: British Medical Journal*, 349. doi:10.1136/bmj.g7348

Bell, B. P. (2016). Overview, control strategies, and lessons learned in the CDC response to the 2014–2016 Ebola epidemic. *Morbidity and Mortality Weekly Report Supplements,65*(3), 4-11.

Betancourt, T. S., Brennan, R. T., Vinck, P., VanderWeele, T. J., Spencer-Walters, D., Jeong, J., ... Pham, P. (2016). Associations between mental health and Ebola- related health behaviors: A regionally representative cross-sectional survey in post-conflict Sierra Leone. *PLOS Medicine, 13*(8), 1-15. doi:10.1371/journal.pmed.1002073

Brew, L., &Kottler, J. A. (2008). *Applied helping skills: Transforming lives.* Thousand Oaks, CA: Sage.

Brewin, C. R., Andrews, B., & Valentine, J. D. (2000). Meta-analysis of risk factors for posttraumatic stress disorder in trauma-exposed adults. *Journal of Consulting and Clinical Psychology, 68*, 748–766. doi:10.1037/0022-006X.68.5.748

Bride, B. E., Robinson, M. M., Yegidis, B., &Figley, C. R. (2004). Development and validation of the Secondary Traumatic

Stress Scale. *Research on Social Work Practice, 14*, 27–35. doi:10.1177/1049731503254106

Brinkmann, S. (2014). Interview. In T. Teo (Ed.), *Encyclopedia of critical psychology* (pp. 1008-1010). New York, NY: Springer.

Brolin Ribacke, K. J., van Duinen, A. J., Nordenstedt, H., Höijer, J., Molnes, R., Froseth, T. W., ... Ekström, A. (2016). The impact of the West Africa Ebola outbreak on obstetric health care in Sierra Leone. *PLOSONE, 11*(2), 1-12. doi: 10.1371/journal.pone.0150080

Bronfenbrenner, U. (1994). Ecological models of human development. In *Internationalencyclopedia of education* (2nd ed., Vol. 3, pp. 1643-1647). Oxford, England: Elsevier.

Centers for Disease Control and Prevention. (2014). Cases of Ebola diagnosed in the United States. Retrieved from http://www.cdc.gov/vhf/ebola/outbreaks/2014- westafrica/united-states-imported-case.html

Charlson, F. J., Diminic, S., Lund, C., Degenhardt, L., &Whiteford, H. A. (2014). Mental and substance use disorders in Sub-Saharan Africa: Predictions of epidemiological changes and mental health workforce requirements for the next 40 years. *PLOSONE, 9*(10), 1-11. doi:10.1371/journal.pone.0110208

Cheung, E. Y. (2015). An outbreak of fear, rumours and stigma: Psychosocial support for the Ebola Virus Disease outbreak in West Africa.*Intervention,13*(1), 70-76.

Cohen, L., &Manion, L. (1994). *Research methods in education* (4th ed.). London, England: Routledge.

Coltart, C. M., Johnson, A. M., & Whitty, C. M. (2015). Role of healthcare workers in early epidemic spread of Ebola: Policy implications of prophylactic compared to reactive vaccination policy in outbreak prevention and control. *BMC Medicine, 13*.doi:10.1186/s12916-015-0477-2

Converse, M. (2012). Philosophy of phenomenology: How understanding aids research. *Nurse Researcher, 20*(1), 28-32. Retrieved from journals.lww.com/nursingResearch online/pages/default.aspx

Cope, D. G. (2014). Methods and meanings: Credibility and trustworthiness of qualitative research. *Oncology Nursing Forum, 41*(1), 89-91. doi: 10.1188/14.ONF.89-91

Corley, A., Hammond, N. E., & Fraser, J. F. (2010). The experiences of health care workers employed in an Australian intensive care unit during the H1N1 Influenza pandemic of 2009: A phenomenological study. *International Journal of Nursing Studies, 47*(5), 577-585.

Creswell, J. W. (2009). *Research design: Qualitative, quantitative and mixed methods approaches* (3rd ed.). Thousand Oaks, CA: Sage Publications.

Csordas, T. J., & Lewton, E. (1998). Practice, performance, and experience in ritual healing. *Transcultural Psychiatry, 35*(4), 435-512.

Darboe, A., I-Feng, L., Hsien-Wen, K., Lin, I., &Kuo, H. (2016). Effort-reward imbalance and self-rated health among Gambian healthcare professionals. *BMC Health Services Research*, 161-169. doi:10.1186/s12913-016-1347-0

Delamou, A., Beavogui, A. H., Kondé, M. K., van Griensven, J., & De Brouwere, V. (2015). Ebola: Better protection needed for Guinean health-care workers. *Lancet, 385*(9967), 503-504.

deMenil, V. P., Knapp, M., McDaid, D., &Njenga, F. G. (2014). Service use, charge, and access to mental healthcare in a private Kenyan inpatient setting: The effects of insurance. *Plos ONE, 9*(3), 1-7. doi: 10.1371/journal.pone.0090297

Denzin, N. K., & Lincoln, Y. (2003). *The landscape of qualitative research. Theories and issues*. (2nd ed.). London: Sage.

Ding, Y., Qu, J., Yu, X., & Wang, S. (2014). The mediating effects of burnout on the relationship between anxiety symptoms and occupational stress among community healthcare workers in China: A cross-sectional study. *Plos ONE, 9*(9), 1-7. doi: 10.1371/journal.pone.0107130

Eckes, E. J. (2016). Educating health care providers in treatment of patients with Ebola Virus disease. *Critical Care Nurse, 36*(5), e8-e13.doi:10.4037/ccn2016814

Engel, N., et al. (2017). Making HIV testing work at the point of care in South Africa: A qualitative study of diagnostic practices. *BMC Health Services Research, 17*(1). Erickson, F. (2012). Qualitative research methods for science education. In *Second international handbook of science education* (pp. 1451-1469). Dordrecht: Springer.

Evans-Lacko, S., & Knapp, M. (2016). Global patterns of workplace productivity for people with depression: Absenteeism and presenteeism costs across eight diverse countries. *Social Psychiatry & Psychiatric Epidemiology,51*(11), 1525-1537. doi:10.1007/s00127-016-1278-4

Fasina, F. O., Adenubi, O. T., Ogundare, S. T., Shittu, A., Bwala, D. G., &Fasina, M. M. (2015). Descriptive analyses and risk of death due to Ebola Virus Disease, West Africa, 2014. *Journal of Infection in Developing Countries, 9*(12), 1298-1307. doi:10.3855/jidc.6484

Fernandes, W. N., & Nirmala, R. (2017). Workplace stress and coping strategies among Indian nurses: Literature review. *Asian Journal of Nursing Education and Research, 7*(3), 449-454. doi:10.5958/2349-2996.2017. 00088.X

Flisher, A. J., Kramer, R. A., Grosser, R. C., Alegria, M., Goodman, S. H., &Greenwald, S. (1997). Correlates of unmet need for mental health services by children and adolescents. *Psychological Medicine, 27*, 1145–1154.

Forster, E. B. (2012). A historical survey of psychiatric practice in Ghana. *Ghana Medical Journal, 46*(3), 25-29.

Frankfort-Nachmias, C., &Nachmias, D. (2008). *Research methods in the social sciences* (7th ed.). New York, NY: Worth.

Glasberg, A. L., Eriksson, S., &Norberg, A. (2007). Burnout and 'stress of conscience' among healthcare personnel. *Journal of Advanced Nursing,57*(4), 392-403. Greenbank, P. (2003). The role of values in education research. The case for reflexivity. *British Educational Research Journal, 29*(6), 791-801.

Greenberg, N., Wessely, S., &Wykes, T. (2015). Potential mental health consequences for workers in the Ebola regions of West Africa - A lesson for all challenging environments. *Journal of Mental Health, 24*(1), 1-3. doi:10.3109/09638237.2014.1000676

Guba, E., & Lincoln, Y. (1994). Competing paradigms in qualitative research. In N. Denzin & Y. Lincoln (Eds.), *Handbook of qualitative research* (pp. 105–117). Thousand Oaks, CA: Sage.

Gustafsson, G., Norberg, A., &Strandberg, G. (2008). Meanings of becoming and being burnout–phenomenological-hermeneutic interpretation of female healthcare personnel's narratives. *Scandinavian Journal of Caring Sciences, 22*(4), 520-528.

Gwaikolo, W. S., Kohrt, B. A., & Cooper, J. L. (2017). Health system preparedness for integration of mental health services in rural Liberia. *BMC Health Services Research*, 17110.doi:10.1186/s12913-017-2447-1

Hann, K., Pearson, H., Campbell, D., Sesay, D., & Eaton, J. (2015). Factors for success in mental health advocacy. *Global Health Action*, 8. doi:10.3402/gha. v8.28791

Harris, N. (2001). Management of work-related stress in nursing. *Nursing Standard, 16*, 47–52.doi:10.7748/ns2001.11.16.10.47.c3122

Heidegger, M. (1889–1976). Criticized Husserl's theory of phenomenology and attempted to develop a theory of ontology that led him to his original theory of Dasein, the non-dualistic human being.

Heidegger, M. (1992). *History of the concept of time: Prolegomena* (Vol. 717). Indiana University Press.

Howlett, M., Doody, K., Murray, J., LeBlanc-Duchin, D., Fraser, J., & Atkinson, P. R. (2015). Burnout in emergency department healthcare professionals is associated with coping style: A cross-sectional survey. *Emergency Medicine Journal, 32*(9), 722. doi:10.1136/emermed-2014-203750

Hsiung, P. C. (2008). Teaching reflexivity in qualitative interviewing. *Teaching Sociology, 36*(3), 211-226.

Hughes, P. (2015). Mental illness and health in Sierra Leone affected by Ebola: Lessons for health workers. *Intervention, 13*(1), 60-69.

Husserl, E. (1967). The thesis of the natural standpoint and its suspension. In J.J.

Kockelmans (Ed.), *Phenomenology* (pp. 68-79). Garden City, NY: Doubleday-1913. Ideas. London; George Allen and Unwin, Republished 1962, New York: Collier.

Husserl, E. (1982). *Ideas pertaining to a pure phenomenology and to a phenomenological philosophy: First book, General introduction to a pure phenomenology.* (F. Kersten, Trans.). Boston, MA: Kluwer Academic Publishers.

Ivey. A. (2000). *Development therapy: Theory into practice.* North Amherst, MA: Micro Training Associates.

Jalloh, M. F., Li, W., Bunnell, R. E., Ethier, K. A., O'Leary, A., Hageman, K. M., ... Marston, B. J. (2018). Impact of Ebola experiences and risk perceptions on mental health in Sierra Leone, July 2015. *BMJ Global Health, 3*(2), e000471.

Jarvis, E. (2013). How to write results for a qualitative phenomenological study. Retrieved from http://www.ehow.com/how_8540568_write-results-qualitative phenomenological-study.html

Johnson, S. R. (2014). CDC sends Ebola help to struggling healthcare workers in Africa. *Modern Healthcare*, 0010.

Jonsson, A., &Halabi, J. (2006). Work related post-traumatic stress as described by Jordanian emergency nurses. *Accident and Emergency Nursing,14*(2), 89-96. Jordan, T. R., Khubchandani, J., &Wiblishauser, M. (2016). The impact of perceived stress and coping adequacy on the health of nurses: A pilot investigation. *Nursing Research and Practice*. doi:10.1155/2016/5843256

Joyce, M. P., Kuhar D.& Brooks, J. T. (2015). Notes from the field: occupationally acquired HIV infection among health care workers – United States, 1985 -2013. *Morbidity and Mortality Weekly Report, 63*, 1245.

Khalid, I., Khalid, T. J., &Qabajah, M. R. (2016). Healthcare workers emotions, perceived stressors and coping strategies during a MERS-CoV outbreak. *Clinical Medicine & Research, 14*(1), 7-14. doi:10.3121/cmr.2016.1303

Koh, M. Y. H., Chong, P. H., Neo, P. S. H., Ong, Y. J., Yong, W. C., Ong, W. Y., . . . Hum, A. Y. M. (2015). Burnout, psychological morbidity and use of coping mechanisms among palliative care practitioners: A multi-centre cross-sectional study. *Palliative Medicine, 29*(7), 633-642. doi:10.1177/0269216315575850

Koinis, A., Giannou, V., Drantaki, V., Angelaina, S., Stratou, E., &Saridi, M. (2015).The impact of healthcare workers job environment on their mental-emotional health. Coping strategies: The case of a local general hospital. *Health Psychology Research, 3*(1), 12-17. doi:10.4081/hpr.2015.1984

Li, L., Chang li, W., Ru, D., Yi, L., Jue, C., Zonggui, W., ... Li, C. (2015). Mental distress among Liberian medical staff working at the China Ebola Treatment Unit: A cross sectional study. *Health & Quality Of Life Outcomes, 13*(1), 1-6. doi:10.1186/s12955-015-0341-2

Lund, C., Boyce, G., Flisher, A., Kafaar, Z.& Dawes, A. (2009). Scaling up child and adolescent mental health services in South Africa: Human resource requirements and costs. *Journal of Child Psychology & Psychiatry, 50*(9), 1121-1130.

Lund, C., Myer, L., Stein, D., Williams, D., &Flisher, A. (2013). Mental illness and lost income among adult South Africans. *Social Psychiatry & Psychiatric Epidemiology, 48*(5), 845-851. doi:10.1007/s00127-012-0587-5

Manuwa, S. (1971). Introduction. In R. Schram (Ed.), *A history of the Nigerian health services* (pp. xiii-xxi) Ibadan, Nigeria: Ibadan University Press.

Mateen, F. J., &Dorji, C. (2009). Health-care worker burnout and the mental health imperative. *Lancet,374*(9690), 595-597.

Matiti, M. R. (2005). The cultural lived experience of internationally recruited nurses: A phenomenological study. *Diversity & Equality in Health and Care, 2*(1), McCall, D. (2009). Ecological/systems approaches to school human development. *Internal School Health Network.*

McCulloch, J. (1995). *The African mind: Colonial psychiatry and the African mind.* Cambridge, UK: Cambridge University Press.

Merriam, S. B. (1998). *Qualitative research and case study application in education.* San Francisco, CA: Jossey-Bass.

Mokaya, A. G., Mutiso, V., Musau, A., Tele, A., Kombe, Y., Ng'ang'a, Z., ... Ng'ang'a, Z. (2016). Substance use among a sample of healthcare workers in Kenya: A cross-sectional study. *Journal of Psychoactive Drugs, 48*(4), 310-319. doi:10.1080/02791072.2016.1211352

Moll, S. E. (2014). The web of silence: A qualitative case study of early intervention and support for healthcare workers with mental ill-health. *BMC Public Health, 14*(1), 1-23. doi:10.1186/1471-2458-14-138

Moore, K., & Cooper, C. (1996). Stress in mental health professionals: A theoretical overview. *International Journal of Social Psychiatry, 42,* 82–89. doi:10.1177/002076409604200202

Morse, J. M. (1994). *Designing funded qualitative research. Handbook of qualitative research* (2nd ed., pp.220-235). Thousand Oaks, CA: Sage.

Morse, J. M. (2006). Insight, inference, evidence, and verification: Creating a legitimate discipline. *International Journal of Qualitative Methods, 5*(1), 1–7.

Moustakas, C. (1994). *Phenomenological research methods.* Thousand Oaks, CA: Sage Publications, Inc.

Mugisha, J., De Hert, M., Stubbs, B., Basangwa, D., &Vancampfort, D. (2017). Physical health policies and metabolic screening in mental healthcare systems of sub- Saharan African countries: A systematic review. *International Journal of Mental Health Systems,* 111-117.doi:10.1186/s13033-017-0141-7

Musa, B. M., John, D., Habib, A. G., &Kuznik, A. (2016).Cost-optimization in the treatment of multidrug resistant tuberculosis in Nigeria. *Tropical Medicine & International Health, 21*(2), 176-182. doi:10.1111/tmi.12648

Myers, D. (1994). *Disaster response and recovery: A handbook for mental health professionals.* Rockville, MD: Centre for Mental Health Services.

Oexle, N., Ajdacic-gross, V., Müller, M., Rodgers, S., Rössler, W., &Rüsch, N. (2015). Predicting perceived need for mental healthcare in a community sample: An application of the self-regulatory model. *Social Psychiatry and Psychiatric Epidemiology, 50*(10), 1593-1600. doi:10.1007/s00127-015-1085-3

Oyebode, F. (2006). History of psychiatry in West Africa. *International Review of Psychiatry, 18*(4), 319-325. doi:10.1080/09540260600775397

Pack, M. (2014). Vicarious resilience: A multilayered model of stress and trauma. *Affilia, 29*(1), 18-29.

Padayacheya, U., Ramlalla, S., &Chipps, J. (2017). Depression in older adults: Prevalence and risk factors in a primary healthcare sample. *South African Family Practice, 59*(2), 61-66.

Paladino, L., Sharpe, R. P., Galwankar, S. C., Sholevar, F., Marchionni, C., Papadimos, T. J., ... Stawicki, S. P. (2017). Reflections on the Ebola public health emergency of international concern, part 2: The unseen epidemic of posttraumatic stress among health-care personnel and survivors of the 2014-2016 Ebola outbreak. *Journal of Global Infectious Diseases, 9*(2), 45-50. doi: 10.4103/jgid.jgid_24_17

Parpia, A. S., Ndeffo-Mbah, M. L., Wenzel, N. S., & Galvani, A. P. (2016). Effects of response to 2014-2015 Ebola outbreak on deaths from malaria, HIV/AIDS, and tuberculosis, West Africa. *Emerging Infectious Diseases, 22*(3), 433-441. doi:10.3201/eid2203.150977

Patton, M. Q. (1990). *Qualitative evaluation and research methods* (2nd ed.). Newbury Park, CA: Sage.

Patton, M. Q. (2002). *Qualitative research & evaluation methods* (3rd ed.). Thousand Oaks, CA. Sage Publications.

Pearlin, L. (1989). The sociological study of stress. *Journal of Health and Social Behavior, 30*, 241-256.

Pearlin, L. (1995). *Some conceptual perspectives on the origins and prevention of social stress*. Paper presented at the Workshop on Social Stressors, Personal and Social Resources and their Health Consequences, sponsored by the National Institute of Mental Health Office of Prevention and Special Projects, Bethesda, MD.

Pearlin, L. (1999). The stress process revisited. In C. Aneshensel & J. Phelan (Eds.), *Handbook of sociology of mental health* (pp. 395-415). New York, NY: Kluwer Academic/Plenum.

Pearlin, L., Morton, A., Lieberman, M., Menaghan, E., &Mullan, J. (1981). The stress processes. *Journal of Health and Social Behavior, 22*, 337-356. Retrieved from http://www.asanet.org/

Pearlin, L., &Skaff, M. (1996). Stress and the life course: A paradigmatic alliance. *Gerontologist, 36*(2), 239-247. doi:10.1093/geront/36.2.239

Pearlman, L. A., & Mac Ian, P. S. (1995). Vicarious traumatization: An empirical study of the effects of trauma work on trauma therapists. *Professional Psychology: Research and Practice, 26*, 558–565. doi:10.1037/0735-7028.26.6.558

Peredaryenko, M. S., & Krauss, S. (2013). Calibrating the human instrument: Understanding the interviewing experience of novice qualitative researchers. *Qualitative Report, 18*(43), 1-17. Retrieved from www.nova.edu/ssss/QR/ calls.html

Pescosolido, B. A. (2013). The public stigma of mental illness: What do we think; what do we know; what can we prove? *Journal of Health and Social Behavior,54*(1), 1-21.

Petrites, A. D., Mullan, P., Spangenberg, K., & Gold, K. J. (2016). You have no choice but to go on: How physicians and midwives in Ghana cope with high rates of perinatal death. *Maternal and Child Health Journal, 20*(7), 1448-1455. doi:10.1007/s10995-016-1943-y

Petti, S., Protano, C., Messano, G. A., & Scully, C. (2016). Ebola virus infection among western healthcare workers unable to recall the transmission route. *BioMed Research International*.

Pietkiewicz, I., & Smith, J. A. (2014). A practical guide to using interpretative phenomenological analysis in qualitative research psychology. *Psychological Journal, 20*(1), 7-14. doi:10.14691/cppj.20.1.7

Polit, D. F., & Beck, C. T. (2006). *Essentials of nursing research: Methods, appraisal, and utilization* (6th ed.). New York, NY: Lippincott Williams & Wilkins.

Potter, A. W., Gonzalez, J. A., & Xu, X. (2015). Ebola response: Modeling the risk of heat stress from personal protective clothing. *Plos ONE, 10*(11), 1-10. doi: 10.1371/journal.pone.0143461

Qiao, Z., Chen, L., Chen, M., Guan, X., Wang, L., Jiao, Y., . . .Zhai, X. (2016). Prevalence and factors associated with occupational burnout among HIV/AIDS healthcare workers in china: A cross-sectional study. *BMC Public Health, 16*. doi:10.1186/s12889-016-2890-7

Raab, K., Sogge, K., Parker, N., &Flament, M. F. (2015). Mindfulness-based stress reduction and self-compassion among mental healthcare professionals: A pilot study. *Mental Health, Religion & Culture,18*(6), 503-512. doi:10.1080/13674676.2015.1081588

Radeke, J., & Mahoney, M. J. (2000). Comparing the personal lives of psychotherapists and research psychologists. *Professional Psychology: Research and Practice, 31*, 82–84. doi:10.1037/0735-7028.31.1.82

Rubin, H.J., & Rubin, I. S. (1995). *Qualitative interviewing: The art of hearing data*. Thousand Oaks: CA, Sage Publications, Inc.

Rugema, L., Krantz, G., Mogren, I., Ntaganira, J., &Persson, M. (2015). "A constant struggle to receive mental health care":

Healthcare professionals acquired experience of barriers to mental healthcare services in Rwanda. *BMC Psychiatry*, 15. Retrieved from https://search- proquest.com.ezp.waldenulibrary.org/docview/1779578279? accounted=14872

Sadowsky, J. (1999). *Imperial bedlam: Institutions of madness in colonial Southwest Nigeria*. Berkeley, CA: University of California Press.

Saini, R., Kaur, S., & Das, K. (2016). Stress, stress reactions, job stressors and coping among nurses working in intensive care units and general wards of a tertiary care hospital: A comparative study. *Journal of Postgraduate Medicine, Education and Research,50*(1), 9-17. doi:10.5005/jp-journals-10028-1184

Saldaña, J. (2015). *The coding manual for qualitative researchers* (3rd ed.). Los Angeles, CA: Sage Publications.

Sandelowski, M. (1986). The problem of rigor in qualitative research. *Advances in Nursing Science, 8*,27-37.

Saxena, A., & Gomes, M. (2016). Ethical challenges to responding to the Ebola epidemic: The World Health Organization experience. *Clinical Trials (London, England), 13*(1), 96-100. doi:10.1177/1740774515621870

Schram, R. (1971). *A history of the Nigerian Health Services*. Ibadan, Nigeria: Ibadan University Press.

Scott, S. D., Hirschinger, L. E., Cox, K. R., et al. (2009). The natural history of recovery for the healthcare provider "second victim" after adverse patient events. *BMJ Quality & Safety, 18*, 325-330.

Selamu, M., Thornicroft, G., Fekadu, A., & Hanlon, C. (2017). Conceptualization of job- related wellbeing, stress and burnout among healthcare workers in rural Ethiopia: A qualitative study. *BMC Health Services Research*, 171-11.doi:10.1186/s12913-017-2370-5

Shane, J. W. (2007). Hermeneutics and the meaning of understanding. *Theoretical Frameworks for Research in Chemistry/Science Education*, 108-121. Shenton, A. K. (2004). Strategies for ensuring trustworthiness in qualitative research projects. *Education for Information, 22,* 63-75.

Shoji, K., Bock, J., Cieslak, R., Zukowska, K., Luszczynska, A., &Benight, C. C. (2014). Cultivating secondary traumatic growth among healthcare workers: The role of social support and self-efficacy. *Journal of Clinical Psychology, 70*(9), 831-846. doi:10.1002/jclp.22070

Sukeri, K., Betancourt, O. A., & Emsley, R. (2014). Lessons from the past: Historical perspectives of mental health in the Eastern Cape. *South African Journal of Psychiatry, 20*(2), 34-39. doi:10.7196/SAJP.568

Taghva, A., Farsi, Z., Javanmard, Y., Atashi, A., Hajebi, A., &Khademi, M. (2017). Stigma barriers of mental health in Iran: A qualitative study by stakeholders of mental health. *Iranian Journal of Psychiatry, 12*(3), 163-171.

Troy, P. H., Wyness, L. A., & McAuliffe, E. (2007). Nurses' experiences of recruitment and migration from developing countries: A phenomenological approach. *Human Resources for Health, 5*(1), 15.

Turner, D. W. (2010). Qualitative interview design: A practical guide for novice investigators. The Qualitative Report, 15(3), 754-760. Retrieved from http://www.nova.edu/ssss/QR/QR15-3/qid.pdf

Tuohy, D., Cooney, A., Dowling, M., Murphy, K., & Sixsmith, J. (2013). An overview of interpretive phenomenology as a research methodology. *Nurse Researcher, 20*(6), 17-20. Retrieved from journals.lww.com/nursingresearchonline/pages/default.Aspx

Umubyeyi, A., Mogren, I., Ntaganira, J., &Krantz, G. (2016). Help-seeking behaviours, barriers to care and self-efficacy for seeking mental health care: A population- based study in Rwanda. *Social Psychiatry and Psychiatric Epidemiology, 51*(1), 81-92. doi:10.1007/s00127-015-1130-2

Valandra, V. V. (2012). Reflexivity and professional use of self in research: A doctoral student's journey. *Journal of Ethnographic & Qualitative Research, 6*(4), 204-220. Retrieved from www.jeqr.org

van Manen, M. (2014). *Phenomenology of practice: Meaning-giving methods inphenomenologicalresearch and writing.* Walnut Creek, CA: Left Coast Press. van Manen, M. (2017). Phenomenology in its original sense. *Qualitative Health Research, 27*(6), 810.

Verial, D. (2013). What is random purposeful sampling? Retrieved from http://www.ehow.com/info_8595186_random-purposeful-sampling.html

Vygotsky, L. (1978). Interaction between learning and development. *Readings on the Development of Children, 23*(3), 34-41.

Walden University. (2013). Institutional Review Board (IRB) for ethical standards in research. Retrieved From http://researchcenter.waldenu.edu/Application-and- General-Materials.htm

Waldrop, D. P., Kramer, B. J., Skretny, J. A., Milch, R. A., & Finn, W. (2005). Final transitions: Family caregiving at the end of life. *Journal of Palliative Medicine, 8*(3), 623-638.

Weiss, B., & Amie, A. P. (2017). Barriers to global health development: An international quantitative survey. *PLoS One, 12*(10). doi: 10.1371/journal.pone.0184846

World Health Organization. (2013). Department of communicable disease surveillance and response. Retrieved from http://www.who.int/csr/resources/publications/surveillance/plague.pdf

World Health Organization. (2015). *Health worker Ebola infections in Guinea, Liberia and Sierra Leone: A preliminary report.* Geneva, Switzerland: Author. Retrieved from: http://www.who.int/csr/resources/publications/ebola/health-worker- infections/en/

World Health Organization. (2016). Retrieved from http:apps.who.int/ebola/current- situation/ebola-situation-report.2016

Appendix A

Invitation Letter

Dear Participant,

This Letter is to ask your permission to participate in a research project. The purpose of the study will be to use a qualitative approach to explore the lived experiences of healthcare workers in Freetown, Sierra Leone about their mental health symptoms while providing treatment to Ebola virus patients. As part of this purpose, the rationale for doing this study is to provide more in-depth, and helpful information on mental health symptoms experienced by healthcare workers during the 2014 and 2015 Ebola outbreak. There will be no composition to participate in this study. However, there will be refreshments available during the interview sessions. The findings of the study may help identify specific intervention strategies to enable healthcare workers to cope with stress or any mental illness.

The interview will run from 30 to 45 minutes with me as the researcher in which I will ask questions about your experiences of providing care for the Ebola virus patients in the 2014 and 2015 outbreak. Also, your thoughts on your mental health and stress, and how it may have been affected by the epidemic. The interview will be audio recorded and transcribed into a word document. You will be asked to provide feedback on the transcript for accuracy and also provide input on the findings of the study for accuracy and conclusions reached.

The transcript will only be accessible to me. If you decided to remove yourself from the interview, all data collected from you would be immediately destroyed. Your participation is strictly voluntary. There is no foreseeable risk in this study. However, if you feel uncomfortable during the interview, you may remove yourself from the study.

There is no penalty or accountability for removing yourself from the study. Information provided in this study will remain confidential. The data will be locked in a secure location and will not be traced back to participants who participated in the study. Further, all participants names will be coded, and no identifiable name will be in the presentation.

I am a doctoral student at Walden University in Minneapolis, Minnesota. This research is part of my doctoral study for the completion of my doctorate in clinical psychology. I am working on the direction of my chairperson, Dr. Patricia Loun (patricia.loun@waldenu.edu) Clinical Psychology Program. If you have any questions regarding this study, please contact me at 916-470-1816 or guy.taylor@waldenu.edu.

This project has been reviewed by the Walden University IRB procedures governing your participation in this research. Your signature signifies your willingness to participate in this study. Please return this document with your signature within the next four days, if possible. Thank you very kindly for your sincere effort to participate in this study.

Sincerely,
Guy Taylor

I have read the above letter, and I understand the nature of this research. I give my consent, and I would like to be a willing participant.

Participant's Signature --
Researcher's Signature--

Appendix B

Interview Questions

The following interview questions pertain to Research Question 1Type it out

1. Describe for me your mental health when treating patients with the Ebola virus disease.
2. Did you experience any signs or symptoms of any mental health issues?

The following interview questions pertain to Research Question 2

3. Please describe your lived experiences of stress related to providing care for the Ebola virus disease patients.
4. What specific factors do you feel affects your stress levels that may affect how you provide care for patients with the Ebola virus disease?

The following interview questions pertain to Research Question 3

5. What was your lived experienced of mental health treatment you were provided when treating patients with the Ebola virus disease?

6. Do you agree with or disagree with the use of adequate mental health care for healthcare workers during an epidemic and why? Please elaborate on your answer.
7. What specific support do you think will be helpful in relieving stress when working with highly infectious patients, such as the Ebola virus disease patients?

Appendix C

Human Subject Training Certificate

Certificate of Completion

The National Institutes of Health (NIH) Office of Extramural Research certifies that **Guy Taylor** successfully completed the NIH Web-based training course "Protecting Human Research Participants."

Date of Completion: 07/21/2018
Certification Number: 2857283

GUY TAYLOR's
CURRICULUM VITAE

916-470-1816 | tayl7g@aol.com | guytaylorccpc@gmail.com | POBOX 340982, Sacramento, CA 95834

EDUCATION

Doctor of Philosophy, Psych, Specialized in Clinical Psychology, Walden University, Minneapolis, Minnesota 2020- Present

Dissertation: Perspectives of Sierra Leoneans Healthcare Workers' Mental Health During the Ebola Outbreak

Master of Science in Psychology, Specialization in Applied Psychology, Walden University, Minneapolis, Minnesota – Conferred in 2014

Master of Science in Clinical Psychopharmacology, Chicago School of Professional Psychology, 325 N Wells St, Chicago, IL 60654 - Current

Bachelor of Science in Psychology, California Coast University, 925 N Spurgeon St, Santa Ana, CA 92701 -2008

License Psychiatric Technician, Mission College, 3000 Mission College Blvd, Santa Clara, CA 95054 - 1997

PANELS & PROFESSIONAL ASSOCIATIONS

American Psychological Associations
International Safety for Children Affairs
Psychological Counseling for Adolescents
Quality Home Care for the Elderly
Professional Book Publication ISBN# 978-1-4836-2834-9

Amazon, Google, Barns & Noble, IRF, Xlibris

Title: We become what we think about: Guy O. Taylor, Master of Science in Psychology. This book talks about the power of one's mind. It addresses several areas of human motivations. In addition, this book addresses the power of spiritual meditation. Published in 2012.

SKILLS SET

- Team Building & Performance Improvement & Cultural competency
- Dual diagnosis/Referral Services/Drug testing
- Mental health Delivery System/HIPPA/Privacy laws/Code Ethics
- Law Enforcement Training (graduated from the academy in January of 2003)
- SPSS system usage
- Medically disoriented offenders evaluations/Keyhea process)
- Counseling, Spiritual Coaching, resource management
- Individual Counseling & Development Plans/Recovery Support IDP
- Conduct Psychotherapy (CBT/DBT). Stress management workshops
- Health Care Administration & Health Care Delivery Systems
- Audit Psychiatric medical files
- Longer term recovery Support services/discharge planning
- Educational Health and Social Services Evidence Based Programs
- Consulting/Workshops/Educational instruction
- Educational Health and Social Services Evidence Based Programs
- Consulting/Workshops/Educational instruction
- Strong Vision and Mission Planning
- Cognitive Behavioral Training
- Contract Negotiations & Strategic alliances
- Strategic Prevention Framework Plan (SPF)/evaluations
- Logic models/Team Building
- Media Campaign/ Business Operations

- Physical Fitness and Meditation Training
- Emergency preparedness ambulatory services ARNG
- Cultural competency/Cultural excellence
- Conflict Resolution
- Policy & Research Procedure Development

PROFESSIONAL HISTORY

Psychology Intern: Nebraska Mental Health Center/ M.S., PLMHP, 4545 86th St., Lincoln NE 68526, 2019

- Provide psychological services to diverse clients

Licensed Psychiatric Tech: California Department of Corrections / Repressa, CA 95671 2007-Present Assist in providing basic general behavioral and psychiatric nursing care to inmates in the correctional setting.

- Dispense psychotropic medications to inmates with mental illness.
- Conduct daily rounds and monthly summaries of patient's behavior.
- Conduct daily therapeutic groups to increase the self-esteem of the inmates.

Mental Health Counselor: California Counseling and Psychological Services, 2007 -2012.

- Work under the direct supervision of LCSW, MSW, and psychologists.
- Provide CBT, WAIS, and Personality Assessment to clients.
- Conduct clinical assessment on the mentally ill and court referral clients.

Medical Technical Assistant/Peace Officer: California Medical Facility-Salinas Valley

- Monitored yard activities as well as encouraged inmates to participate in groups.

- Conducted cell extractions and administered medication to inmates.

Licensed Psychiatric Technician: California State Prison-Pelican Bay. 1999-2000

Assist in providing basic general behavioral and psychiatric nursing care to inmates in the correctional setting.

- Dispense psychotropic medications to inmates with mental illness.
- Conduct daily rounds and monthly summaries of patient's behavior.
- Conduct daily therapeutic groups to increase the self-esteem of the inmates.

Psychiatric Counselor: Crestwood Manor -1993-1999 (408) 275 -1010

- Monitored adult psychiatric clients grooming and hygiene.
- Managed daily schedule of client activities.

COMPUTER SKILLS

XP-MICROSOFT WORD, EXCEL, WORD, WORDPERFECT, POWER POINT, PUBLISHER, MICROSOFT OFFICE, OFFICE

XP, QUICKBOOKS, INTERNET SEARCH, ENGINES, WEBPAGE DESIGN, E-MAIL, MICROSOFT OUTLOOK, VARIOUS COMPUTER SKILLS.

OVERVIEW

Twenty plus years successful experience providing, mental health delivery systems, project development leadership, human resource management, working with legal, worked in State Government, and the County level, and Non- profit Corporations, and for profit Corporations.

Dynamic, strong psychopharmacological skills, and a track record of performance in office organizational psychology team approach, to drive organizational improvements, and implementation of best practices. Capable of resolving complex and multi task responsibilities, sound knowledge of logic modules, capacity building, planning and implementation, strategic prevention framework, (SPF) , work with coalitions, establish community partnerships.

CPSIA information can be obtained
at www.ICGtesting.com
Printed in the USA
BVHW041032150819
555976BV00008B/181/P